Table for One

Thoughts of a Round the World Backpacker

Table for One

Thoughts of a Round the World Backpacker

Chris Ambrose

ISBN 978-0-9564473-0-2

Published by Chris Ambrose

ambrosebook@googlemail.com

Cover design by Mark and Bekki Tomkins at Aubergine 262

www.aubergine262.com

Cover photography © Chris Ambrose

Printed and bound in Peterborough

A note from the author...

That's right, I'm *even* referring to myself as an author now.

Hi, I'm Chris. It's nice to meet you. I never intended to write a book about this - it just sort of...happened. (That's what writers of these types of books are supposed to say isn't it?) But thanks to a few suggestions from various people, and the monotonous routine of job hunting — the email updates that I sent home from my travels have turned into this. So here it is; a book about my backpacking adventure around the world.

All the events in the following pages happened as I tell them, and all the places and people mentioned are real (except *maybe* if I mention any people after a night of 'goon' drinking — these people's existence cannot necessarily be verified). Where I have mentioned names, these are *almost* all real, but where I have changed names, or when I haven't referred to people by name, this isn't an editorial judgement - I'm just bad with names and probably forgot them. So I'm sorry for that.

Anyway, I now invite you to sit back and enjoy some armchair travelling...

Prologue

"And how long do you want to spend in Australia?"

"Erm…" I paused briefly as I took a sweeping look across the map of this vast country that lay before me, before hesitantly replying. "Three months…?"

"Okay." She marked it down with alarmingly casual administrative efficiency.

"And how long would you like in New Zealand?"

What? Is that it?! You can't ask me an important question like that and just accept my answer can you? How the hell should *I* know how long I should spend in Australia - I've never been! I'm clearly buzzing from my recent completion and resulting escape from twenty years of education, and now with the prospect of an impending worldwide adventure at my fingertips I *surely* can't be expected to be making rational decisions like that without at least a *little* guidance.

There must be some kind of quiz they can inflict on me to see whether I have any clue as to why that period of time would be suitable for my visit – my visit to a country I knew *absolutely nothing* about, except that I wanted to be there, and for some inexplicable reason, and in that brief moment, I had decided that the ideal time was three months.

But no. That *was* it. Those two and a half seconds of 'careful deliberation' had defined my location for a quarter of my upcoming year. There was no 'are you sure?' no 'do you have any idea what you're going to do with yourself whilst you're out there?' not even a sharp, quizzical look to give me the time and opportunity to rethink my genius plan.

And now it appeared that there wasn't *even* the flexibility to change my mind, as before I knew what had happened she had effortlessly filled this important data into an online planner. I *think* she may have even circled the '3' that she now had written down on her note pad. If that wasn't setting it in stone, then I didn't know what would be.

Maybe I should explain…

It was a cold, dark December night, and… well, I'm lying. It was a warm, sunny June afternoon, and I was wandering aimlessly up Southampton High Street having recently finished my university course. I was crossing the road by the Guildhall complex when I noticed the STA travel shop.

Actually that's a little misleading; I knew it was there, and I had every intention of going in it once I had finished with university, so it wasn't really a great shock when I strode confidently through the door.

"Hello! Can I help you?" said a bright, cheery voice from behind one of the desks.

And that was it. I was lured into the customer seat, and mercilessly drained of all my money…

Okay, okay, so that's not strictly true either. I told the lady behind the desk that I wanted to go round the world (which to be honest I found quite amusing, because it's not every day you walk into a shop and ask to buy something as large and vague as a massively long and expansive worldwide adventure. I mean, it's not like I was enquiring about swimming pool entrance fees, or the measurements for a curtain rail - this was a *much* more significant purchase). She, on the other hand (presumably based on the fact that she works in a travel shop and gets requests like that all day long) didn't flinch, and simply showered me in brochures and leaflets about…well, the world.

She then proceeded to tell me about a 'Round the World' evening that they were hosting the following Wednesday evening. She said that there would be presentations about different aspects of travel. I said that it sounded interesting. She then said that there would be free alcohol. I said I would be there.

So the following Wednesday I set off, accompanied by my friend Dan (who I'd roped along for company, but to be honest didn't really need a huge amount of persuasion once I had mentioned the alcohol inclusion) and we strutted down the street, having both donned our finest silk gowns and diamond slippers, and headed for the bright lights of the city. Luckily Wednesdays were a regular night out, so to have our pre-drinking provided for us was a real bonus.

What followed were an entertaining couple of hours about round-the-world adventure, featuring first-hand accounts, slideshows, and motivational cheering at the relevant moments. The beer flowed, and so did the energy and enthusiasm of the staff as they shared their experiences of travelling. They even did a short geography quiz (that I secretly enjoyed *far* too much) *and* I won a bottle of mid-priced wine. They really were selling us the dream. Dan even won an eco-bag! It was for sure, a crazy night.

I then returned to the travel agency a few days later, this time with my debit card. This was serious. I had looked over a few brochures and maps, and had roughly decided on where I thought I wanted to go, and now it was time to finalise it.

Now I had two main objectives when it came to travelling; I wanted to be in Australia for Christmas, and I wanted to go around the world, as in – leave to the east, and return from the west. Simple.

Forty minutes. That's *all* it took. I walked in, and then forty minutes later I walked out. It was ridiculous. I mean I've been known to spend longer tying my shoelaces! Yet in that time I had planned eight months of my life, spent more money than I had *ever* spent in one transaction before, and I even had time to spare in which to make several inappropriate comments about suitcases.

You could have called it an efficient visit, or you could say it was reckless. I guess I would find out in November, which was when I was now firmly booked to depart on my round the world adventure…

* * *

And in the months more previous to November, a traveller of much unsuspectance did secure pennies most righteous, for these formed the pounds sovereign that would hence fund such a trip - a trip of much great magnitude, fortitude, and latitude. Then the traveller did proceed forth to pack bags - not one, but two. And in the said bags did compile socks most numerous in quantity and colour, and whence was done, the beholder did rejoice...through the means of a chuckle.

The hour then came for judgement and flight. And the hour was 9, and the minutes 40 in number...

Chapter 1

Scheduled Flights and Sleepless Nights
Thoughts of an Unsuspecting Traveller

I've done it. I'm on the plane. That's got to be commitment. I mean I could try and get off now and throw the several thousand pound trip away...but I couldn't risk losing all that face. And it would be a lot of face.

No, I think I'm safe now. To an extent anyway. There is the argument that boarding the plane is the easy part, other than the 'moral' or 'philosophical' approach, which suggests the first step is the hardest. Having said this, it is a little disconcerting that the seat next to me does appear to be the only empty seat on the plane. I also find it strangely worrying that the airline 'Qantas' does not feature a 'u' after the 'Q'. This may seem like a strange point to take issue with, but it does go against everything I was taught through all those English lessons, and therefore I fear that entrusting this airline with my life could be risky. Or worse, I've had a bad education.

Day 0

At least I presume it's day zero. That may of course just be the fashionable name for it. It is late in the day, and through the laws of time I will be losing much of tomorrow to B-list films and novelty food packaging. Don't get me wrong, I'm fascinated by the technical arrangement that is the economy in-flight food service, and I will no doubt watch the films three times each, but I'm British, and we're told that us Brits have a talent for moaning. So we'll call this day zero, and that will be the end of it.

Day 2

Yup, I skipped a day, but then I wasn't sure when it started anyway. Also, I'm new to this journal business and it will probably take a while to get the hang of it. Anyway, here goes...

I arrived at Bangkok's fancy new airport in a daze of possibility. Oh, and with scruffy hair from where I'd tried to sleep. I managed to withdraw some Thai Baht, despite the constant harassment from local taxi-touts trying to lure me into their captivity. I then managed to find the bus I wanted that would take me into the city. This was going well.

The journey was quite long as every inch of Bangkok's road network is filled with vehicles, all of which seem to take road signals and markings as merely a suggested guideline.

After over an hour of inching through the congestion, by which time it was dark, we finally pulled up in a busy street and everyone got off. I took this as a sign and followed, and having acquiring a map from a nearby tourist information shop, and with another newly arrived backpacker in tow, we managed to find our way around, and I was soon at my hostel.

I'm staying in a stylish en-suite room with a bed and a television that half picks up a collection of inaudible channels. The bed is quite big – not a king size, or even a queen size…so probably a prince size, or a senior-assistant-to-the-royal-family size. The en-suite is very novel however - It's a wet room. I'm not sure if this is intentional, but it *is* nevertheless fashionable. The toilet is the centrepiece, strategically positioned diagonally across the centre with the shower directly above it.

After settling into my new accommodation I wandered around the nearby streets for a bit, before heading to bed around 10pm as I hadn't really slept for a day. It didn't work. The room was hot (having only mastered the air conditioning today) and I was very awake, not helped by someone trying to break into my room during the night. Lovely. On three separate occasions there was frantic shouting, banging and kicking on my door as someone claiming to be from the hotel tried to lure me out in my sleeping attire, presumably to rob or kill me. If I'm honest I didn't fancy any of that this early on in my trip, so I stayed silently in bed until he got fed up and left me alone. Given the walls were so thin I could hear everything very clearly, and this guy didn't seem to pick on any other rooms which I *knew* to have occupants, so I decided it must have been a welcoming act, and that they do this to new guests to 'break them in'. I can't say it was hugely appreciated, but I finally got to sleep around 5am.

The next morning I was up around 10am, had my inclusive 'continental' breakfast (a bit of dry bread and fruit) and wandered off with my bag to enjoy the sights and smells of Bangkok life.

Day 2 (evening)

That's right, I'm getting fancy with my day divisions.

I have just spent two hours re-kindling my love of reading. Quiet! Not since the four-month torture of 'The Hobbit' when I was fifteen have I ventured into a book with such commitment.

Danny Wallace's 'Yes Man' is genius. The idea of saying 'yes' at every opportunity is so simple, and made me consider adopting such a scheme myself, although in reality if I did say 'yes' at every offer I think I may have to turn Buddhist, buy half of Bangkok (albeit at a very reasonable rate) and I would probably have been massaged to destruction, given the constant barrage of offers encountered in such a place. It has however made me reflect upon how a series of pressure induced 'yeses' across a thirty minute period in June led me on this adventure...and how organising eight months of your life in half an hour can be risky.

Anyway, I'm off out now to search for food (as my trouser are falling down) and before a little man who calls me 'Kiss' comes and tries to whisk me off to experience some 'true Thai culture'...

Day 3

Last night was interesting. It started with a meal, escalated into note passing, and ended up with an invite to a Thai 23rd birthday party.

I went out into the street near my hostel to find somewhere to eat. I soon found a nice looking restaurant and after requesting a 'table for one', I sat down with a local 'Chang' beer. I was then subjected to a weird routine of what I can only assume is some form of 'restaurant initiation' by the waitress, but would probably constitute harassment back home. She kept calling me 'sexyboy' and hitting me with a menu. I assumed this was how it worked round here, so I tried to be polite about it.

After I had received my meal, *another* waitress showed up giggling, and handed me a note on a serviette. It read "Will you be my friend?" As I was six thousand miles from home and everyone I knew, this was probably one of those

5

occasions where I *could* have probably done with a friend, but I was actually pretty contented on my own. I dubiously replied (not knowing who this note was from) saying "ok...?", and soon, and without being given an option, I was moved to a table with a Thai girl that had giant fingernails.

Jenny had just finished university in Bangkok and wanted to go into banking. Her English was quite good, although to be honest I wasn't really listening, as her long glittery red, white and blue fingernails were still concerning me.

While we were chatting, two little ladies came up to our table and started playing Ronan Keating's 'When You Say Nothing At All' on the guitar. They had done this to several tables around us, and were clearly irritating guests. It was to their surprise then, and the surprise of the others around, that having finished playing the song at our table, I then took the guitar and played a more accurate version of the song back at them. This got me a clap. Travelling life is good.

We then went off to a few bars, where at one such establishment I met a sixty year old American man who had been travelling for forty years. It made my two days seem a little pitiful really. Still, we chatted extensively about current affairs and world politics, and as the beer flowed I started to really get into the travelling way.

I think my deep discussions with the American annoyed Jenny though, and I ended up having to give money to a little flower girl to make peace. That was a forty pence expense I hadn't budgeted for!

Anyway, with Jenny back on side, we moved on. She told me it was her 23rd birthday tomorrow, and invited me to her party. I wasn't all that keen. She was an odd combination of shy but quite forward, and with the constant fear that she might have the same 'equipment' as me (having had these warnings drilled into me) and that I really don't want a Thai bride, I made my excuses, dropped her with her barmaid friend who was working at one of the bars, and went back to bed. Via the second half of Chelsea versus Newcastle. It was 0-0. I didn't get to sleep until 5am again (bloody jet lag) despite a now fully functioning air conditioning system.

I got up quite late today (you know, not having any commitments and all that) and wandered to the river, where I went on a bridge and took my first photos! Having satisfied this important task I moved on, and spent half an hour precariously negotiating my way across some busy, lawless roads before finding myself at the National Museum of Bangkok. I took a few more photos of the highly colourful and intricately decorated buildings and then began strolling around it.

I ended up spending quite a while there, partly due to there being so much to see, and partly down to the vast maze of galleries that meant I was reasonably lost for much of the time. I soon realised that despite it being very busy, I was pretty much the only non-Asian, and I also appeared to be the only one in shorts. I suddenly wondered if this was a custom that I was not adhering to. Not a problem! I was wearing zipped-off, zip-off trousers, and so I stopped and whipped out my...

...leg attachments (nearly had you) from my bag, and began to attach.

Without realising it, it appeared that this act had turned into quite the attraction. I looked up to see I had drawn a crowd of around seven people, who, once I had completed the tricky zip manoeuvre, changed their fascination into spontaneous applause! I saw a Thai man with a mobile phone that turned into a television with a pull out aerial...but zip off trousers are obviously a true Western phenomenon!

I had a brief conversation with a small Thai man yesterday;

"Where are you from?"

"London."

"South-East London?"

"Err, no, North-West." (He probably thought I was being cheeky.)

"Ah! Preston!"

Nailed it.

Day 4

Dear diary, tonight I'm feeling...Nah, not really! Last night was weird. You think you have eventful evenings when you're at university...and *then* you go travelling.

It started in the normal way; "Table for one please!" and soon I was tucking into a nice beef-noodle concoction, before wandering off into the night. I then (out of nowhere) heard a "Kiss, Kiss!" As I had now established that this means 'Chris' in Thai, I looked up to see Jenny summoning me to her party. With my inability to say "sorry, I've got to be up early for work." (Subtle dig at you full time workers? No? Sorry.) I headed over.

I then encountered a full set of over-the-top gay, ladyboy and 'alternative' Thai folk, plus an absolutely hammered Swede (who initially wanted to "thump me into the ground" but was later concerned for my well-being) and a Tanzanian guy, who was super-chilled out. He didn't really speak, but his look and demeanour suggested that he was probably Samuel L. Jackson, especially in the hat he was wearing.

I rapidly became the novelty act of the party, and was soon featuring in many photographs with various dubious 'women' much to my hesitance. I was even passed a phone to speak to someone. Funnily enough – don't speak Thai in person; don't speak it on the phone. Anyway, they plied me with free alcohol and 'clink-ed' my glass every twelve seconds while the twenty-eight year old, overtly homosexual man (who looked fourteen) kept rubbing my shoulders. Not quite the travelling dream.

Luckily a random guy called Joe (from Reading) showed up, and alerted me to the fact that most of these 'girls' probably 'weren't all they seemed'. A conclusion I was rapidly coming to as well. I was cautious of them before, now I felt mild panic.

Anyway, most of the group slipped off and I somehow ended up in a club with Samuel L. Jackson, talking to a hairdresser (there seems to be a lot of them about - which may come in handy around late March) and an Irish girl, whose boyfriend was getting his arse well and truly kicked at pool by a Thai 'girl' who was only using one hand. The rest of the night was uneventful...

Today I met Joe at 1pm as drunkenly arranged last night. We chatted in a bar as Thailand's favourite tourism boost - 'The Beach' was playing on repeat on the television screens above.

We then wandered around Bangkok before arranging to meet up again in the evening. We were going to see where the night took us. It took us past Jenny and co.

Unfortunately the road our hostels were on meant we had to walk past the bar where she worked to get anywhere else, and despite a strategic and highly inventive plan to avoid her (walking quickly) she caught sight of us. Dammit!

We were summoned in and submitted to more bizarre Thai hosting, involving dubious hand movements, but also some quite tasty complimentary barbecued chicken strips. Well there's no gain without pain, and those wooden slatted seats were bloody uncomfortable.

Luckily after a few whiskeys (I know, I thought you had to be at least sixty as well...) I suggested we played pool. This worked out brilliantly as the 'girls' didn't want to play pool (maybe they were real girls...?) so we agreed to 'meet them later'. Four days in and already avoiding people. Not good.

So the two of us went off and played pool and had a fun night away from dangerous fingernails.

It's now my last night in this swanky prison cell, and it will feel strange to finally put on some clean underwe...I mean leave. I still haven't tried urinating while showering, despite the obvious design features that urge me to do it. It would remove any issues of back-splash...but no, it would be a bad habit to get into.

Day 6

Yesterday I moved to the fancy hotel up the road. Fridge, working television, chairs, balcony – I'm in over my head! But it's okay, it won't last for long. This was the starting place for a group trip that would see us travel through South East Asia.

In the evening we met up as a group for the first time. Everyone seemed very nice and on the same wave length, which promised well for the trip ahead.

After the early introductions and necessary administrative business were out of the way, we went for dinner at a nice restaurant, then onto an Irish bar with a Thai band playing classic Canadian hits. Well what else would you expect? We then went back for a relatively early night. I got to sleep at 5am. *Again.*

The next morning we were up early for a group breakfast, and then we went to see the Grand Palace. It was gold and shiny. We also got to see the 'Great Emerald Buddha', which was in fact very small, and made of jade.

I then went on to track down the 'Big Reclining Buddha'. He's *very* big. *And* reclined. This restored my faith in local descriptions. I also learnt from a street man on my way to the reclining Buddha that they burnt the king's sister last week. I think something may have been lost in translation there, but whatever was going on it must have been significant, given all the memorabilia and the masses of groups around the Palace.

I still find it amazing how you can walk for five minutes from the tourist hotspot of Khao San Road and lose all the tourists. When I'm on my own I still appear to be quite the novelty, and get stared at constantly, and if I wave, I get huge cheers and laughter in response. If only I'd stuck around to whip off my leg attachments…

Day 7

That evening we gathered in the hotel lobby with all our bags for the short taxi ride to the station. Here we stocked up on some provisions before boarding the night train north to the city of Chiang Mai. There was certainly an air of excitement amongst the group as we set off to begin our travelling adventures…

Chapter 2

Spring Rolls and Rafting Poles
Thoughts of a Hill-Trekking Elephant Tamer

Day 12

We arrived in Chiang Mai around three hours late. The sixteen-hour train journey was quite an experience, with a three-course meal, lots of card games, an interesting bunk arrangement (complete with cockroaches), and even some sleep, despite more or less being sent to bed at 10pm. Using the toilet/hole in the floor was however a challenge.

I spent our first day in Chiang Mai wandering around the town and exploring, while other group members did a cooking course, had a massage...or did nothing.

A few of us then went over to a five star hotel and swam in its (freezing) fourth floor swimming pool, and used its steam room, sauna, and jacuzzi. I had tracked on a map how we had got there in the taxi-truck, and so we navigated our way back through the lively bustling streets of the city that is laid out around a square river (don't ask how that works) that borders the city, and is decorated by occasional city wall ruins.

That night we went to pick up any kit we needed and had a group meal, before meandering through the famous night markets, trying desperately to avoid the 'frog women', who walk around in their strange outfits scratching the back of little calved wooden frogs with sticks, which apparently made 'frog noises', in a vain attempt to secure a sale. I didn't buy one. No one *else* bought one. I doubt *anyone* in the history of tourism would *ever* buy one. Yet still they persist.

The next day we set off into the jungle hills. We stopped at a market to pick up any provisions we needed, before setting off into the steeper terrain, bouncing around helplessly in the back of the off road trucks.

After a while (and a few bruised arms and legs later) we stopped at a waterfall. It was a hot day, and we were all very keen to take a dip. It was *freezing*! It was also a lot of fun, and standing under the falls gave a nice powerful massage.

We then drove on to the start of our trek. It was indeed very hilly, and after around three hours of trekking through the jungle, swinging on vines and slipping down slopes, we arrived in a clearing at the hill tribe village where we would be staying that night. It was pretty large, with huts scattered right across the valley, and a collection of animals wandering free around the village. We were given a bizarre tour by some of the excitable resident children, before helping to make some spring rolls that formed part of our dinner. If you don't like rice, chilli and pineapple - in Thailand – you're screwed*.

Thailand is the world's largest producer of pineapple, and the world's biggest exporter of rice you know!

It was a thoroughly enjoyable and much-welcome dinner, and as a group we were all bonding, and happily chatting together in our exciting new surroundings.

After dinner we sat around a fire, and our leader, John, pulled out a guitar! He said he couldn't play and so handed it to me to do the honours. Just before this, another guide started playing Ronan Keating's 'When You Say Nothing At All'. I'm starting to think this song is the Thai National Anthem.

A couple of hours later, and after a lot of rummaging around with head torches, we all sorted ourselves out in our various huts and went to bed. It was a very solid floor, and freezing cold. I got two hours sleep.

The next day we got up and had a strangely continental breakfast (What? No rice?!) and packed up our stuff before setting off into the hills once again. It was even more up and down today, but the rolling jungle hills were very dramatic.

We stopped at one point, where we were surrounded by water buffalo (with cow bells on!) and the guides showed us some 'stick trick' puzzles as some light relief from the heat and humidity.

We trekked for around four hours, eventually arriving at a few small huts by a river. We were tucking into some lunch (rice) when out of nowhere...well actually from around the corner and *in* the river - came elephants! We finished off the rice and noodle soup accompaniment, and then patted the large grey animals until it was time to ride them!

Each elephant took two passengers on the dodgy wooden seats, and a guide on the head. Our elephant was an angry male ten year old (named Boris...we all had to name them apparently) who kept dipping irrationally, and blowing its trunk in our faces. It was quite an experience - and bum numbing too. Whether intentional or not, the convoy of elephants began to get competitive and a race seemed to develop, albeit a very slow one, but there was still plenty of anger and trunk blowing thrown in for good measure. The up and down ride through rivers and up very steep river banks eventually left us with a short hike to our next camp – a small selection of huts by the river.

After ditching our belongings in the bamboo huts that were suspended in the air (and the wide cracks meant you could see all the creepy crawlies beneath you) we went into the river (which was again, *very* cold) and tried repeatedly to cross it. After around half an hour we began to realise (probably a little slowly) that we were fighting a losing battle, as the current was too strong and the rocks very sharp, so we gave up and had dinner instead.

Having finished eating another fine rice-based jungle concoction, we gathered around the fire where we played games whilst being entertained by the bizarre drunken/opium enhanced moves of one of the guides, who seemed to suggest he wanted a job in the British government...but spoke little English, and smoked everything he touched. He probably wouldn't be viewed as the ideal candidate, but was impressive in his own...*special* kind of way. He did teach us the elephant song though!

"Chang, Chang, Chang, Chang, Chang!!!" There were actions too, and these made the song even *more* exciting. I guess you had to be there.

We then got cold and tired, and so went to bed at the ridiculous hour of 9pm. Again, it was freezing and very uncomfortable. Four hours sleep max.

The next morning we put on our Speedos, as today we were travelling by bamboo raft! After breakfast we packed up our gear once again, but this time put everything in plastic bags, and then we headed down to the riverbank to board our transport. The rafts were literally long bits of bamboo tied together, with a bamboo tripod at one end to hold the bags. We sailed serenely down the river for three hours, with six of us on each raft in a line, plus a guide at the front and back. We had the crazy opium-mashed guy at the rear, singing constantly about his love of elephant pee pee, and the occasional shouting out to water buffalo we passed along the river bank; "How are you tomorrow?"

We took it in turns to help the raft along with 'oars' (bamboo poles) and we stood up most of the time (the water was very cold and bamboo isn't the most

17

comfortable). However we had to sit down sometimes as we hit rapids. We all got very wet. In one instance we got lodged under a rock and nearly capsized. Frantic people re-positioning and adjustment saved us, but even the bags got wet. Some would say we could have drowned, but those people are drama queens. We probably *did* nearly drown though. Despite this it was all good fun.

We arrived at our finishing point quite drained, but were soon drying off and sat in front of our freshly prepared lunch - noodles! It was then back on the trucks for the trip back to Chiang Mai, all very tired, but having had a great trek in the jungle hills, and a thoroughly enjoyable start to our South East Asian adventure...

* * *

Now I wasn't planning on writing about the past few days until I was away from here, but I think I need to fill some time...

On Sunday we arrived back at our hotel in Chiang Mai, exhausted, but having really enjoyed the three-day trek. Some of the group planned on going back to the 'posh' hotel for the jacuzzi, while others fancied a Thai massage. I wanted to go back to my room and get cleaned up.

I picked up my bag from storage and went to my room. I had a very satisfying shower, scrubbing off three days of grime, dirt, river water and facial hair. I then began to sort out my bag. I suddenly realised that some of the pockets of the bag were open, and things had been moved around. After a closer inspection I realised I couldn't find a drawstring bag containing my camera, mp3 stick, playing cards, and a few other odd bits that I didn't have room for, or didn't need for the trek. I emptied my bag but it wasn't there. F*ck it. This put a bit of dampener on a really good few days. I went down to reception and checked my email. I didn't have the motivation at that point to reply to any just then.

The evening picked up as the group met for dinner, and we ventured off into the busy, market-filled lights of the town, having told the guide about the problem and him telling me to go to the tourist police office in the morning. I was frustrated at the thought (or principle) of not having music (which I had spent hours compiling prior to departure) for the rest of the trip, but looked on the positives of the fact that many of the group were by now unwell, and were hurting from all the trekking, while I felt fine, and was very grateful for it.

Don't get me wrong, I don't take pleasure in other people's misfortune and suffering, but it does help put things into perspective. Something I would gain a lot of in the coming days. I also had the benefit of now having a lighter load to carry around, seeing as that I could now ditch all those sodding chargers and adapters!

The next morning I got up early to sort out the bag business, boarding a tuk tuk (my first one!) to the tourist police. I was feeling alright this morning, but our guide had told me to report it to the police, even just as a warning to others who might be leaving items at the hotel.

I arrived at the place and was ushered inside where I filled out my details and information on a claim form. They then asked if they could go to the hotel. That was fine, I even got to ride in the back of a police car!...it wouldn't be the last time that day.

On the journey, what I can only assume to be a trainee officer seemed to be chatting me up, asking me lots of 'friendly' questions about myself, and participating in a strange winking exercise. The four of us arrived at the hotel, and after a chat between the police and the hotel staff at reception in Thai, they asked to see my room. Yep, come on up! I made them walk. I was on the fourth floor. In retrospect this may have cost me. Upon arrival they immediately began searching the room, opening draws, checking under mattresses, and combing the general vicinity. It was kind of exciting. Excitement that wouldn't last. They soon asked me to empty my bags. I was only too happy to oblige (other than the fact I would have the inconvenience of having to re-pack it afterwards). I shouldn't have worried. I wouldn't get to do that.

I took out my wash-kit, clothes, and a few other bits before turning my attention (under instruction) to my day bag, and began emptying that. While my back was turned the officers carried on muttering, before one of them drew out from apparently nowhere…a small…drawstring bag…

My initial reaction was of great joy mixed with confusion. My belongings had been returned! Although why when I had just emptied my bag in front of them and *I* hadn't found it I couldn't understand. Where and when had they got hold of it? Had I been robbed and it been returned? Had that moody ar*e-hole at reception screwed me over? But I didn't have time to think about these things. Quickly I felt the mood darken. Someone had been through my bag, yet these people were looking at me as if *I* had just stolen from *them*.

Later suspicions would arise over the possible replacement of the items by hotel staff/police, as well as stories from other travellers about corruption and deals between hotel staff and police in Chiang Mai. I have also since been told about stories of how they love catching foreign travellers with drugs (hence the ransacking of my room) but obviously my lack of a substance abuse problem had disappointed them, so they chose a different, less ethical tactic.

But there was no time for those thoughts to cross my mind yet. Right now I was stuck in something very strange, and feelings of confusion filled my mind, but this was nothing to what the looks on the officer's faces suggested I should be feeling. They seemed to think I was guilty. Guilty of…attempted insurance fraud? Guilty of lying.

* * *

This was not good. I could see it in their eyes. I couldn't understand it though. My bag had been opened and things taken – I had shown them this. What had they been saying to the hotel staff when they arrived? Had some arrangement been done? To be honest it was only later that these thoughts set in. Maybe it was a degree of naivety that I was shielded by at this point, but whatever was going on, it wasn't good and I started to worry. They began muttering a lot, and I kept hearing the word 'lie' repeated over and over. Worry turned seamlessly into mild panic.

They mentioned something about 'signing the form' and having to arrest me. This was bad. Very bad. The worst start to December since I played an angel in my reception Christmas school play and I messed up the opening line. At least I got a toy car out of that episode. I don't think I was in line for a Christmas present from the Chiang Mai tourist police today.

The officers led me off to the police car, and we headed back to the tourist police station. It would be fair to say that conversation was less casual on this trip, and the air was full of tension. I wish that damn bag and its contents were still missing now. I wish I had never experienced a tuk tuk and gone to the police. I wish I'd just let the stuff go. I wish they hadn't bloody screwed me over!

We arrived at the police station again, and I was sat down. What followed was a series of loosely English interrogations, interspersed with photographs of me and my belongings…and the occasional 'tourist shots' with other officers beside me. All very weird. It was made clear to me that the seriousness of the situation stemmed from me having signed the crime report declaration. The declaration that stated that if the information I supplied was false, I faced a fine and/or imprisonment.

Shit.

But it had been true! Where was that glorious British line that mentions 'to the best of your knowledge at the time of writing.'?! How was I to know they would return it? It's just not conventional criminal activity to return it. Maybe they had realised that my camera wasn't expensive, and that a whistle and a pack of cards weren't worthy of the black market. They could have at least had the decency to just chuck them. There was certainly no need to set me up. Besides, I had a train to catch!

A man walked over to the desk in front of me where my possessions lay, as if taunting me.

"How many mega pixels?" he barked, holding up my camera.

"Err, 7.2…?" I replied, sheepishly.

He studied the camera, and then me, and then retorted angrily, "8!"

Crap. Was a technicality like that going to get me a fine? Or worse, was being 0.8 out going to get me sent to jail?

I was not feeling good, even when they brought me out some water and a fish meal. Once again they had misjudged me. Not only was I *not* the master criminal they had hoped for, but also they evidently thought I was the type of person who enjoyed seafood under intense interrogation pressure.

A drunk man, possibly German, stumbled in, and through minimal speech indicated that all his money and cards had been stolen from his wallet while he was in his hotel room (by flinging it open in the officer's face). The incomprehensibility of his exchange meant the officer asked if the man could come back tomorrow. I wish I could come back tomorrow, I thought. Or maybe not at all.

A very important and senior looking officer then stood before me. His English was not clear at all, but his feelings were.

"You lie! Why you lie!?"

"I didn't!" I spluttered.

"You think Thai police are weak? You think you can get away with it? You Brits are all the same!" He was glaring at me very menacingly.

That was a little xenophobic I thought. "No!" I cried out in desperation. I had seen some of 'Vinnie Jones' – World's Toughest Cops' – and the one in Thailand was not pretty.

"You disrespect king! You go to prison for three years!"

Dammit! I knew exactly how important the king was round here by all the flags, shrines, and current bombings and airport barrages that were going on…but how the hell had I offended him? Had my photos been of such a low standard that I was possibly damaging future tourism?

One of the female officers came up to me and suggested I wrote an apology letter. I wasn't sure what I was supposed to apologise for but I was willing to try anything to sort this out quickly. I felt like I was eight years old. 'I'm very sorry for...' Eventually I was told I had to go to another police station after reports of the incident had been written up. I wasn't sure up to this point if I had been officially arrested. Now it seemed clear. I was escorted to the police station where I was led into a cell.

Twenty minutes I spent in there. It was rubbish. It's hard to explain what goes through your head in that situation, but the thoughts were dark. They then led me to an office where they took more details and I heard mutterings about 'court' and 'punishment' becoming more prominent, and soon I was led back into the cell, with a 'should be court tomorrow'. They took my fingerprints, and then slammed the door. It was 2.30pm. And that's where I stayed for the next twenty-one hours.

Chapter 3

From Cow Bells to Prison Cells
Thoughts of an Unsuspecting Prisoner

The cell is roughly four metres square, and sits in the middle of a selection of smaller cells, with three further cell doors that lead out to the police station. There is a rotting wooden desk and chair outside the cell where the fingerprints are done.

There are strip lights that glaze the cells in a constant haze of light, twenty-four hours a day. One of the side cells appears to be full of crates of beer, while others have boxes in, or very dusty hi-fi and computer components.

In the corner of my cell is a raised-wall section that houses the hole in the floor/toilet, and a tap and bucket. There is a constant smell of excrement. Across from my cell I can see a thin strip of daylight from one of the small meshed windows at the top of a smaller cell. The walls are stained with fingerprint ink hand marks and messages scrawled by prisoners. Most are in Thai, but a couple of lines are in a form of English, some mildly religious. One bold scribble on the side of the toilet wall reads; 'I Remenber'.

The floor has ripped lino on it, and in the corner where I write this is a wicker-style beach mat, two dirty blankets, and two dirty cushions. The cell is bordered by black iron bars, framed by white, message-engraved walls.

My first night in captivity wasn't much fun. It was cold and all I had on was a t-shirt. I spent the first few hours standing against the cell wall, trying to work out why and how I had ended up here. I felt pretty numb. There was a Thai person in the cell too. He kept having loud conversations with family members through the series of cell walls and doors.

At 4pm a group of six women and eight men (all Thai) were led into the cell block. The women were put into a smaller side cell, while the men were put in with us. They were laughing, joking, and smoking. It made a change from the smell of urine. They all had their phones out, calling people, and photographing their big night out. They didn't communicate much with me, but I did establish that they had been arrested for gambling.

A few hours later (by which time I had now slid down the wall, and was now sitting, shivering on the hard floor) dinner was pushed through the cell bars. It consisted of a set of two small plastic bags, one with mushy rice, and the other with a discoloured curry sludge in it, elastic-banded together. It wasn't enticing. I would see a lot of these in the coming days.

A few more hours passed, and then suddenly a man was hurried through the outer cell doors…carrying my bag! This was an exciting moment. Being in that cell was worse than

27

watching paint dry. At least when you're watching paint dry, something is happening...(the paint is drying).

The bag was placed just outside of the cell. For hours I didn't touch it. I'd been told that someone would pack up my bag (from the sprawling mess of luggage left by the police raid) but I wondered how much of the stuff would actually make it. And where was my day bag? I had also put clothes into the hotel laundry service the evening before. A lot of clothes. I was sure *they* wouldn't have made it.

In the end, I went for it. The nothingness was destroying me. My negative thoughts were not comforting. By reaching through the bars I unclipped the hood and loosened the draw-string toggle. On the top was a polythene bag with a pile of neatly folded, clean laundry, beneath which was my day bag. Success! This guy had packed more efficiently than me! I managed to withdraw my clean, fresh-smelling fleece, and whipped it on to suppress the shivering. This was without doubt the highlight of the day.

At 10pm the cell warden came in and ordered out the Thai gambling collective. I'd see them in court. It was now just me, the other guy, and a lot of bags of rice. I decided I should try and get some sleep and indicated to my cell 'buddy' that I would like one of the blankets and cushions. He responded by promptly setting up a double-bed style formation. Erm. Okay. Not really what I had in mind. I cautiously crawled in one side. The blanket did little to soften the floor, and the Thai person kept moving about and resting various limbs on me, intentionally or otherwise... He smelt like cat biscuits. I hate the smell of cat biscuits. It was horrible. I may have had around half an hour of sleep that night.

At 3am I couldn't take it anymore. I was cold, uncomfortable, and unnerved. I got up, grabbed a cushion, and moved to the other side of the cell, where I managed to pull out my book from my bag. I sat on the cushion and read. I read for six hours straight. I've never done *anything* for six hours straight before. I can't even remember the last time I slept for that long. Certainly not since being in Thailand. By the time the Thai group returned for fingerprinting and the breakfast bags were shoved through the bars, my rear end was well and truly numb. From the cell floor you'll understand.

Last night I slept in a bed that was wider than it was long. I was out of breath by the time I had negotiated my way across the three pillows to get my glass of cold water, and to adjust the personal air conditioning system with the digital remote control. I had a dream (during my seven hour sleep, that's right - SEVEN hours!) that I had to get a train to London, but I had forgotten my young person's railcard.

I've spent the last week facing the prospect of a prison sentence, whilst being stuck, isolated from the outside world in a cell, but now it's low-cost public transport that dominates my concerns.

I had been told that someone might have been coming to see me from the embassy at eight o'clock, so I set this as a target. Eight o'clock came and went…but no one else did.

Finally, just before eleven, I was summoned. I was led out of the cell, through the doors of the police station and into the company of another man. I was then escorted outside (daylight!!) and into an open backed truck that was surrounded by mesh where I was locked in. These sort of trucks are used as taxis in Chiang Mai, but this had a less comfortable metal-slat bench arrangement, and the mesh-covered sides and padlocks gave a less…holiday feel to this one.

I was driven for around twenty minutes, arriving quite rattled after the aggressive, bumpy ride, at what I presumed was the court building (no one had spoken to me or told me anything since early afternoon yesterday.) The driver got out…and walked off.

Two hours later, having remained locked in the cage and having passer-bys staring at me like a caged animal, the man returned…and we drove off?! We stopped again after a confusing ten minutes at some sort of medical centre, where the driver got out and muttered, "Wait here". What else was I supposed to bloody do?! I was locked in!

Around ten minutes later he returned, and we set off again. We arrived at another building after another short but violent trip. Here I was released from my mobile cell, thoroughly bruised and confused. I was led up some steps and into the building, where I was (once again) locked in a large holding area. Also in there were the Thai gamblers club.

I was hastily passed a mobile phone through a gap in the cage door, where an Aussie accent greeted me — the tour company operative, called Andy. This was the first proper English I'd heard in over twenty-four hours, and it came as some relief. It was then that I discovered that the British Embassy and my family were unaware of my situation, which was a little disconcerting (as I was minutes from being sentenced) but they assured me that they were getting on the case now.

After about half an hour, the gamblers and myself were summoned to the court room, where we then waited. I had one of the tour guides named Tony there to help me translate. After a guard had rattled on in Thai for twenty minutes, I got passed another phone. It was my dad. It was a reassuring thirty seconds. Now people knew. I then got called to the back of the court room, where, on the other side of the grilled-wall was an English man! A *real* Englishman. One of the most English, Englishmen I had ever met. It was a really positive few moments. He was a consulate from Chiang Mai, and with his Thai translating associate, had arrived here in less than thirty minutes after being told about my situation. I've never been so pleased of being British, and respectful of the British Embassy. I now had a good solid team around me at this hugely crucial moment.

Soon after, having seen no sign of a judge, an officer walked in with our written reports with orange slips attached. It appeared that these were our punishments. I was led back to, and locked in the holding area again, while the team tried to decipher my fate. Eventually, after a lot of confusion it seemed I had a five hundred Baht fine (£10) and a one month prison sentence. F#*@!

* * *

I paid the fine there and then, and a few minutes later, two hundred Baht and a receipt were returned to me. Apparently I got a discount for 'immediate payment'. This seemed stupid. It wasn't a bloody holiday reservation! But I had more pressing issues – prison beckoned. They also chose this moment to hand me a brown envelope with leaflets on 'How to survive in prison abroad' as well as some letter writing paper. How thoughtful.

There was a period of frantic phone calls and enquiries into how much money I had on me to 'negotiate' (bribe) my way out of the sentence. They suggested that eight to ten thousand Baht (£200) might be the rough figure. I didn't really care, I wanted out. In the meantime I had to be returned to my cell (a police van had already been sent) and leave my fate in other people's hands...hoping they could resolve this before the next van was organised to take me off to Chiang Mai Prison. I was led away and driven back to my cell, and locked in again. I would end up spending the next forty-seven hours in that confined space.

After about an hour, Tony appeared at the bars. He told me that I had been relinquished of my prison sentence, and I would be sent to immigration for deportation instead. I sighed the biggest sigh of relief I had ever sighed in my limited history of significant and over-emphasised sighing.

"And how much do I have to pay?" I asked. (Not particularly caring whatever the sum.)

"Nothing, because you are a student."

This was by far the best (and most ridiculous) student discount I have ever had. Of course it could be argued that I am technically no longer a student, but putting unemployed didn't feel right. The irony was not lost on me though. Tony then offered to get me some food. Legend. I hadn't eaten in over a day. I thrust a series of banknotes through the bars, and before long he was back with some food. Some of the best food I had ever tasted. The hours rolled by slowly as I lay on the floor reading, regularly switching positions as my various limbs went numb. I finished the book. I was gutted. Not only had I really enjoyed it, but also its positive theme was an ideal motivator for the situation.

Now I had my bag the same side of the bars as me, I decided to clean myself up a bit. I brushed my teeth, washed my face (my travel soap and wash kit proved ideal for prison life) and I even changed my socks! I also tidied my cell, throwing the unwanted prison food into the bin bag that was hanging on the outside of the bars, and collected up the remains of bottled water that previous inmates had left behind, and lined them up as rations. Then I started reading the book again. I would get halfway through it for the second time during the next day. Then, as a result of my hectic reading and tidying schedule, I lay down, and began to drift in and out of consciousness.

I was rudely awoken a while later by the clanging of cell doors. Suddenly I could hear lots of voices and the scuffling of feet. It looked like I was in for some new cell mates. I lay motionless, as I felt staring eyes fall upon me once again from the other side of the bars. Soon, a group of eight youngish Thai men were in my cell, and quickly gathered around me. Their English was minimal, and I still hadn't quite mastered Thai, and so communication was limited. I did manage to establish that they were all quite drunk, and had in fact been caught drink driving...mopeds.

They seemed quite friendly, and despite the rude interruption to my peaceful captivity, it did pass some time. Eventually, when it was getting on for midnight, we settled down to sleep. I offered around some of my blanket stash (as I was the generous ruler of the cell) and lay back in my thin sleeping bag to embrace the cold, uncomfortable night. Again, despite the available space, the four Thai men (the others seemingly having been released) chose to stay near me (how sweet and thoughtful...) with two of them opting to plant themselves literally on me. One huddled against my bag, while the other had compressed himself between me and the cell bars. And that's how things stayed, until inevitably, morning came, and they were fingerprinted and released. I was not. I was back on my own again.

Wednesday 3rd December

Yes, yes, yes, I'll get back to that in a minute. Right now we're somewhere over the Indian Ocean. I can tell you that with some degree of accuracy because of the selection of maps I have available on my personal touch screen on this flight. Over one hundred television programmes to choose from, forty-odd up-to-date films, thirty-something music albums, and a vast array of games. I have wasted the first half an hour playing 'Who Wants To Be A Millionaire.' It's phenomenal.

They have also brought around plush headphones, night mask and sock packs, drinks, pre-dinner snacks…even a bloody menu for dinner! Amazing. They've even installed a calming red sunset glow to the cabin lighting (that changes as daylight changes, to blues and purples and other exciting combinations in between) and I've got more 'refreshing towels' then I know what to do with. Good work Etihad Airways – and this was the cheap flying option! Anyway, enough talk of luxury – back to life behind bars… (I've just been given metal cutlery!)

Right, so yeah, I was back on my…sorry, I've just had the most delicious piece of chocolate cake. I know I've been using a lot of overtly positive words, but with freedom comes respect for small things, and a great sense of appreciation for them. But I've now *had my cake (and eaten it!) and have selected a music play list to listen to from my touch screen, so I will now get on with the story...*

Wednesday was long. After being abandoned by the drink drivers, I slipped into my routine that was rapidly becoming the norm...as I became...institutionalised?! No that's stupid, it's far too early. I brushed my teeth, shaved, washed my face and tidied the cell. I even started doing some press-ups...but then quickly realised that I wasn't a heavily tattooed prison gang member. So I stopped. I read some more and added to my journal, drawing a picture of my cell view whilst listening to the faint rumble of traffic, the persistent 'meowing' of a cat (from where, I just couldn't work out!) and the incredibly frustrating, incomplete 'cock-a-doodle...' crowing of a nearby cockerel every two minutes. The afternoon dragged on endlessly, with no clues of what might be going on in the real world. The world I was missing. The world I was craving.

I'm currently sitting in what I presume (and hope!) is the departure area at Abu Dhabi airport in the United Arab Emirates. I have just bought a bottle of water using US Dollars, receiving change in UK Pound Sterling and UAE Durhams. I am currently in possession of five different currencies. I have no idea what's going on.

As what I presume was Wednesday evening was drawing in (by now it was getting increasingly difficult to distinguish and keep track of days) I was getting pretty fed up. If they wanted to deport me, then they should bloody hurry up and do it. But apparently they needed the decision signed by the judge, and that is obviously a very long and slow process. (?!) Still, with news that the trusty British Embassy were pushing hard, I had some hope to cling on to.

Late in the evening a familiar thing happened. The clanging of locks and the frantic voices of Thai people having been arrested. This time an assortment of men and women were surrounding me. Two of them in handcuffs! This didn't look good. What had *they* done?! I sat up, and prepared for tonight's prison party.

They were a noisy bunch, not respecting the resident inmate, or my space. One man sat on my blanket (bastard!) and kept leaning against me as he spoke to the women through the bars in the opposite cell. This really pissed me off. I started by edging away, but as the night progressed I resorted to essentially kicking him, in an attempt to regain some personal space (having woken up too many times with an ugly, foul-smelling, snoring Thai face, three inches from mine). That was a major problem with this lot – they were all very loud snorers. So I spent the night, once again, grinding down my hips and knee joints on the concrete floor, while fighting off the unconscious advances of loud Thai men...until morning came, and they buggered off like the rest of them. I was back alone.

Around lunchtime I was paid a much appreciated visit from Tony. He said that they were hoping to get me off to immigration that afternoon, but if not, it would be Monday, as Friday was a public holiday (the king's birthday!) and so the government 'wasn't working'. I'm not convinced it ever was, and I'm sure this was just a convenient ploy by the king to get his revenge on me after I had apparently offended him so badly.

Anyway, I wasn't sure how to take the prospect of another four days in the cell, but he brought me in some food, which helped to soften the blow. I anxiously waited as time ticked on. Then, at 4pm, forty-seven hours after I had been locked in the cell, and just as the next lot of Chiang Mai murderers were being led into my residence – I was summoned! Could this be freedom??!!

No.

Chapter 4

Polos and Post-it Notes
Thoughts of a Hip-Grinding Checkers Player

I was ushered out into the blinding sunlight and into a police truck. We sat in silence as we drove through the city. I was getting excited, as we seemed to be heading towards the airport judging by the signs. But as the smell of escape was starting to waft through the vehicle's air conditioning vents, we turned off into immigration. So close.

I was put into yet another cell. Actually, a cell makes it sound a bit too glamorous. It was essentially a chicken cage packed with people...all of which (as I had become accustomed to) were staring at me. There were lots of food trays and bags lying around. It was like being at the illegal immigrants' summer picnic. I even recognised some of my old cell mates from the previous night. It was such a happy occasion.

Before long, one of the guides showed up, and so did someone from the consulate. It was all looking very promising. After some discussions in the office next to the chicken hutch, I was called over to the gate where I was hit with bad news. Immigration still needed to sort some things, and that couldn't be done until the king had finished his three-day birthday party - on Monday.

So it was back to the cells. I was gutted. Luckily the consort let me phone home for the first proper time since this mess started. It allowed me to hear about all the work that had been going on behind the scenes; the emails, the phone calls, all the effort. And they were the positive thoughts I needed to hold on to, because the next place I went to was certainly not on the *Lonely Planet* recommended accommodation list. I was put into a prison truck transporter along with the rest of *Club Immigration* (except they were herded like cattle into the back, whereas I got the front seat) and we were taken off to the central police station…and the main holding cells.

It would be fair to say that it was grim. We were led down the dark grey corridor (having removed our shoes) and passed other cells. Inmates were pressed up against the doors as the only viewing point, staring sinisterly at us, and especially me, the only tall, skinny white boy in the joint. In these few moments I saw some of the dirtiest looks I had ever seen. I was guided into one of the cells where there were three others inside.

The block consisted of a central passage, with five cells (roughly five metres square each) coming off it. There was no natural light, and the walls were grey with wooden floors. Our cell had bars that bordered the main passage, the others were fully enclosed other than the barred doors, and they were hugely overcrowded.

One of the cells was for women only (except for a small boy who seemed to be in there) who were allowed out into the main passage. The other cells were locked. I sat down on the floor in the corner, and literally hit rock bottom.

I had been warned not to take any valuables into this cell, so Tony took my belongings to the hotel for storage and 'safe keeping'. I had a few wash bits, my sleeping bag, and some water. Oh, and a packet of polos and some post-it notes. These may have saved me.

The outlook was bleak. I felt pretty numb again. It was very hot and stuffy in this airless, loud, and intimidating environment. I didn't know what to do. In the end I cautiously went over to the others in the cell. One was covered in tattoos and looked very stern. All three looked reasonably young. One of them seemed friendlier than the others, and he even knew a few English words.

I decided to try and break the ice by offering round the packet of polos I had been given on my flight here. They took them warily, and I even had to have one, presumably to prove I wasn't trying to drug them. This seemed to soften the mood a bit. (And now at least they had minty-fresh breath. I couldn't risk another cat-biscuit incident after last time.)

I then noticed a checkers board scratched into the wood of the cell floor, and managed to get a game going. Luckily, prison checkers was very similar to home checkers, and so this helped to break the communication barrier, and relieve some of the tension (and pass some time). They used broken bits of polystyrene food container for counters, but I remembered I had some luminous green post-it notes which would be more distinguishable, and so that improved the game, and possibly more significantly, my reputation.

The evening slowly passed, with lots of hand-signalling, helping me to discover a bit more about my cell mates. One was twenty-one, another locked up for three years for boxing. They turned out to be very respectful of their new, unusual companion, and offered me the all too familiar prison food bags, and showed me a bit of cell life (the washing bucket, lying around, scratching the walls, etc…) I was still very glad the other cells were locked up…or that I was locked in (there were some very dodgy looking people in there). Also, if for some reason I had wanted a Thai bride - that would have been the ideal place to get one. I was still quite the novelty.

I wasted some time by collecting the food bag elastic bands and started to make an elastic band ball. Eventually at around 11pm the noise began to die down, and people started to try and get some sleep. I managed some, but it was on and off. Every so often I would be woken by aching joints (I had my fleece on constant rotation to protect whichever bones were bearing the brunt of the hard surface depending on my sleeping position) and the sound of the cell door being opened and banging shut again.

By the time people were waking up early the next morning, our cell number had doubled. There were now eight of us. Immediately I was approached by an Indian looking man in a bright Hawaiian shirt.

"Speak English?" he said, towering over me as I lay semiconscious in my sleeping bag.

"Yes!" I blurted out, probably a little too excitedly. Someone to talk to!

It materialised that Philippe was a fifty-four year old Sri-Lankan who lived in New Zealand, and did a lot of travelling now he was retired. He had arrived in the cell around 1am after being caught with fifty grams of marijuana on the streets of Chiang Mai. He was a very positive, lively person (the drugs probably helped) and his upbeat nature was infectious (as were some of the other new cell members presumably...). Having survived the night and bonded with the others, I had been feeling quite good anyway (given the circumstances) but having someone to chat to certainly furthered that.

A while later I had a special food delivery was pushed through the bars. A little after that I was called for another round of fingerprinting. On my return to the cell I even helped one of the guys with some English reading with the aid of my book, before I was summoned again to the bars where I was handcuffed. This completed the criminal experience, and deep down I had felt that this whole affair had been missing that crucial iron-wrist-detaining edge. So I guess I was now happy, and criminally fulfilled.

I was led out of the cells, sliding along in my socks, to the police offices (aahh, natural light – it burned!!) where I was sat down in front of a desk, surrounded by seven very stern looking uniformed officers. This didn't look good. And then in front of me, on the desk, I noticed three cigarettes, and a stupidly big bag of drugs. Crap. What were they trying to pin on me now?!

Luckily, I realised that they had got the wrong man. This was Philippe's stash! Judging by the looks of confusion around me, they now knew it too, and soon I was hurried back to my cell and de-cuffed. I had enjoyed the walk.

I added some more elastic bands to my ball, then lay back and drifted into a daze. I was by now, quite accepting of my current position, and just sticking it out.

Then, all of a sudden, I was disturbed by a piercing voice at the cell door.

"Chrisofer! You go home now!" What? He repeated it, adding a 'Hurry!'
I couldn't believe it. It was one of the best instruction I had ever had barked at me – and just as I was settling in too...

I frantically stuffed my belongings into my bag, leaving my remaining food and post-it notes for my new cell buddies, shook their hands and left. It was 3pm. I was out!

* * *

44

I spent the afternoon being driven about by Dave (another one of the tour guides) between the hotel and immigration, while he used his 'contacts' to secure my release. I wouldn't be technically released until Monday. I was effectively under house-arrest at the hotel until then. I didn't have access to my money until the other tour guide came back on Sunday, but I had just enough to get by on, despite the court receipt that was needed for my release being in the safety deposit box (it looked for a while like I would have to be returned to the cells until it could be accessed, but he pulled a few strings to save me from an early return to jail) and so I was free! Not even a deportation order. For the first time in a week I could properly change my clothes and lie on a bed.

Two days of dazed wandering around in a haze of freedom followed. I even had a nervy return to the original police station (and cell block) to collect my belongings that had started it all, and a trip to the airport and travel agents to arrange my flights home. Admittedly, there was a bit more to those couple of days than I'm letting on, and I know I've rushed it a bit, but I'm currently about half an hour away from landing at Heathrow airport, having been on fifteen hours of flights and I'm a little tired.

* * *

45

So here I am, three days on from my return to sunny England, having switched thirty degree heat and not a sign of Christmas, to the three degree chills of full-flowing, neon-blinding festive spirit. I remember joking with people after my July hospitalisation incident in Portugal;

'If I can't last a week abroad without getting into difficulties, how am I going to last eight months?!'

Well, the answer to that is, I couldn't. I lasted eleven days.

It turns out that this whole affair came down to a six pound fine. That's about a fifth of a parking ticket. I've also since realised that I've had my head torch pinched. I have decided to let that go.

For now I think I'm just going to settle for a bit of padded sleep and casual English conversation, but I will be returning to the world of travel in the new year, and before long, an unsuspecting barmaid will be hearing...

"Table for one, please!"

Intervalogue

Ah! Bet you've never seen one of these in a book before have you! Well I felt it was necessary...

So I set off on an amazing eight-month round the world adventure...and lasted eighteen days. Not brilliant I think you'll agree, but there were at least a *few* days in those two and half weeks that gave me a real insight into travelling, and a real buzz that I knew I wanted more of.

Back home I had a nice Christmas with my family, and a good ear bashing from my friends. But as the jokes began to subside, and having just missed out on being Christmas number 1 (the local paper brought out an early edition of the following week's paper, and so I wasn't on the front page over Christmas) I began to get a bit frustrated with being at home.

Two months of not being able to earn any money, and not being able to spend any (as I needed it all for my return to the world of travel) meant time dragged on endlessly.

It did give me the opportunity to pack hyper-efficiently, although nine weeks of devising the most space-effective way of folding boxer shorts is never something you should have to go through. Let alone admit to.

However, I did manage to roughly sketch out a new adjusted itinerary, and eventually the date was set. I carefully booked my new outward flight to be on a *very* special aircraft, and I even arranged an exciting activity for my first stopover. Things were looking up, and then it wasn't long before I was back in the departure lounge at Heathrow airport and raring to go...

Chapter 5

Air Miles and Crocodiles
Thoughts of a Slightly More Suspecting Traveller

Day 1

One night in Singapore.

I'm back! That's right, back on a plane. But not just any plane, oh no! This plane has *two* levels. This plane has over *eight hundred* passengers. This plane has a vanity mirror built into the drop-down table. This is the *Airbus A380.*

It's currently minus sixty-four degrees centigrade (although I suspect this may be an outside reading) and we're somewhere over the Poland/Ukraine border, hurtling towards Singapore at over 500mph.

As you may have guessed I've wasted no time in abusing the in-seat entertainment service called 'Krisworld'. I'm going to ignore the obvious spelling error and assume that this flight has been specifically tailored for my personal taste. After all, everyone knows that the most important passengers are given seat 55k...although admittedly I was a little nervous that the 55th row *might* actually be somewhere behind the tail fin, but you'll be relieved to hear that I am in fact safely inside the aircraft, with passengers beside me, in front of me, behind me, above me...and maybe even below me if anyone's sneaked into the luggage compartment.

I also have a window seat, but thanks to Richard Hammond's television experiment, I am confident that should someone fire a recently defrosted Sainsbury's Basics chicken out of a cannon at 200mph at the plane, the fibreglass shell (that currently props up my head) would barely dent. However, before you suggest that I am not a vigilant air passenger, I am partaking in a half-hourly scheduled chicken watch.

You may think that I am a little excited about being on this plane, and you'd be right. I even attempted to take a photo of it from the departure lounge gate window (as others were I might add) but unlike others, I hadn't had the foresight to charge my camera before leaving. Brilliant. I'd been going solo for the best part of nine minutes and I had already cocked up.

Other areas of my preparation have gone smoother though, having received flight socks as anticipated, allowing me to reduce my initial sock intake in the packing phase. I did however select the sweet and sour pork from the flight menu, but they had run out, and so I had to settle for the roast dinner. Strike one for the A380.

There is a constant flow of beverages on offer, but I have opted against the wine as at my current level of excitement I might quite easily drift into the 'drunk' division, and if I lose one more round of 'pub quiz' that could team up with its partner in crime 'disorderly' and I may face a flight suspension that would ruin my A380 experience.

Anyway, enough rambling, I'm going to kick back with some B*Witched...er...Gina G...I mean Ricky Martin...oh god. I think I have inadvertently negotiated my way onto the 90s playlist. Never mind, maybe I'll pick a random seat number and challenge them to a game of battleships. I might choose an 'A' seat, and see if there have been any sightings of out-of-control, high-speed poultry on that side of the plane. Failing that I have sixty-three films to get though before landing...

* * *

It's now...nope, no idea what time zone we're in, but we're somewhere over India. Having had a good twelve minutes sleep I decided it was time to try something else, so I fired up 'Krisworld', won a game of bowling, won $125,000 on 'Who Wants To Be A Millionaire', and taught myself Mandarin. Not bad for twenty minutes work. After this success I decided to stretch my legs, and I took a wander to the back of the plane where I experienced a first; I bashed my hand on the LED soap dispenser. Ok, that wasn't actually a first, I regularly injure myself in confined operational spaces, but I was referring to climbing a staircase* on a plane. Awesome. But I got to the top and didn't know what to do, so I just smiled stupidly at the two air hostesses that were staring at me, and then returned to my seat.

Word of my game show success and linguistic skills must have spread fast, as no sooner had I slid into my executive recliner than a hostess handed me two packs of custom Airbus A380 playing cards. Maybe they're linked, or maybe I'm contracting cabin fever, or just getting a little caught up in 'Chrisworld'.

Few people would be interested to know that the stairs spiralled upwards, anti-clockwise, against usual medieval castle procedure (for reasons too geeky for me to admit to here).

Day 2

I have found my way to the hostel after fighting through the rush-hour traffic on the MRT subway train network. It was very cheap and straight forward, the only difficulty being that I didn't have a small enough bank note for the ticket machine, and when I asked to change it at an exchange desk, the woman said, "No, it lie! This is Singapore!" over and over. She was right, we *were* in Singapore, but she was wrong, I *did* need a smaller note.

Luckily another employee of the train network had more faith in the honesty of the ticket machine, and after changing up some money I was soon on my way. The only other issue to contend with was the reversal of escalator custom - you stand on the left (which makes more sense - drive on the left, overtake on the right) but anyway, I adapted pretty quickly, unlike two elderly Westerners I saw who seemed oblivious to being the only people standing on the right. Bloody tourists. One of them had a ridiculous Hawaiian shirt on too.

Oh, and it's hot here.

* * *

I've just arrived back from Sentosa, an island accessed by a very dramatic cable car ride. The views include an impressive mix of skyscrapers in the CBD, massive container ships and docks, and then this serene tropical island with white sandy beaches and palm trees overlooking...more container ships, and other islands. There were also massive construction projects on the other side of the island to the beaches, adding to the stark contrasts in scenery. It's one of the strangest places I have ever seen. Of course you'll see no evidence of this from me, because my bloody camera still has no battery.

Having wandered through the quiet pathways across the island, I sat on some rocks and strolled on the artificial beach. I then went on a gondola ride up the hill, with more spectacular views capturing the bizarre combination of lush greenery and beaches with full-scale urbanisation. I then took a 'luge' ride back down the hill. This is a small cart-like thing that you race down a hillside. It was great fun. To add to the strange surroundings is the constant heavy downpours that are responsible for my wet feet.

Day 3

Once I had cable car-ed my way back down from Sentosa, I took the MRT to City Hall, and then found my way to the Singapore Flyer (the largest ferris wheel in the world...for now anyway). It was practically empty.

...It's now a lot later on day 3 because I got asked to play pool...and I'm now at Singapore airport waiting to leave. I'm also not wearing any shoes. But that's not important. So back to yesterday...

I boarded my capsule alone. I was going to test how sturdy the windows and doors were to help pass my thirty minutes of encapsulated solitude while the wheel was at its lower stages...but then thought better of it. They might have CCTV to catch me out. And probably just for that reason. So instead I looked out of the windows. Various people I had spoken to about the wheel had pretty unimpressed views of it (or maybe from it...) but I have to conclude that these people are silly.

Singapore has a hugely impressive skyline, and its dramatic, stark contrasts in scenery are fascinating. I was gutted I didn't have a battery-filled camera. Especially as I said I would make an extra-special effort to take pictures on these travels as I've always been rubbish at it.

What also excited me greatly was the Formula One circuit that looped around the bottom of the wheel. Not only that, but once I had been released from my capsule, I walked on it! I was the only one on the pit straight in the middle of a hugely busy and populated city-country. It was quite surreal. I then spent the next couple of hours meandering around much of the track, peering into the empty pit garages and tracing the faded white track markings where the circuit joined normal roadways. It was good.

So good in fact, that after returning to Little India where I was based, and having had some pretty rubbish food and disappointingly little sleep (despite being shattered from two days without sleep) I got up today and went back to the marina area to walk around some more of the track and to go on the wheel again. This time armed with a fully charged camera! I even got a cheaper ticket for flying Singapore Airways, and it was bright sunshine. Very hot. I think I got a bit of a red nose. If it had been two weeks later it would have been perfect and I could have drawn a face on it...because it would have been Red Nose Day. Not because I'm a crazy freelance nose decorator you'll understand. This time I also had fellow capsulites, and being the regular I helped guide them through the views before them.

* * *

So I'm now about to leave Singapore (it only seems like yesterday I arrived...) and will hopefully soon be at my original goal - Australia!

One thing still puzzles me about Singapore. A commonly advertised offer in Singapore is 'one-for-one'. I read something about paying for two and getting the second later. This doesn't strike me as being a hugely worthwhile offer, so I've concluded that these people are just easily impressed.

Day 4

Australia

I've made it! I'm in the land down-under! Brilliant. So, what now?

Actually I almost didn't make it. I got quizzed repeatedly about my reasons for coming here, who I knew, how long I would stay, what I wanted to see, which was my favourite Spice Girl... I thought they were just being pleasant, but no. The four different people who asked the exact same questions were just taking precautions - possibly stemming from a typo on my Australian visa that read 'sex: F'. Stupid STA. Of all the complications I find myself in, I feel my gender has always remained pretty defined.

I didn't fancy being sent back either; I'm bored of planes. The latest two from Singapore were on an Airbus A320. That 60 less obviously means a lot in aviations terms. Luckily they were shorter flights, and I even managed to get some sleep! Not as much as the women either side of me though, even if they had adopted more unnatural sleeping positions than if someone had rendered them unconscious with a large wooden boating oar. My leg bore the brunt of this, being kicked one minute, and used as a pillow the next. The guy in front of me also thought my bag under his seat was his lifejacket. Yeah, good luck trying to float with that...

Anyway, I got the shuttle bus to the hostel, found out I couldn't check in for another five hours and so I dumped my bag and went off exploring.

I ended up sitting in the 'lagoon'. This is Australia's fancy name for an outdoor swimming pool. I think they made it because you can't swim in the sea because of crocodiles and jellyfish. Maybe after a few beers though...

I then ventured into town to find some interweb, and also to try to sort out my first Oz Experience bus. I got chatting to the Swede on the travel desk - by which I mean a lady from Sweden, and not a large orange vegetable (I know it's hot here and I'm a little sleep deprived but there would be no excuse for that).

So I ended up sorting out all my buses to Melbourne, as well as various exciting trips and excursions. It was pretty successful really, even if my bank balance doesn't agree.

Day 5

I've just got back from not going on a scuba diving trip to the Great Barrier Reef. I splashed through torrential rain and got to the boat to find in had been cancelled as a cyclone was hitting Cairns. I mean, c'mon, sort it out Australia.

I've rescheduled for Sunday, but even that may not happen if Mr C(yclone) Hamish decides to stick around.

Despite my disappointment at not being able to scuba dive, I did manage to have an interesting exchange with an old lady on a boat on my way back from my scuba dive rejection.

"Boat not goin' aaahhht?" a voice growled incomprehensively in a thick Aussie accent. (Not that I blame her for this or was particularly surprised by it, after all, we were in Australia, and people do age. I was just caught off guard.)

"No, because of the cyclone. They've closed the harbour." I replied knowledgably, even though I was just regurgitating the information I had just been told - and she was on a boat in the harbour, so probably knew anyway.

"Neither's that one." she point-nodded at a dodgy looking boat on the other side of the 'finger' (gangway). "It's goin' up the creek!"

I was puzzled. She had either just contradicted herself (she *was* pretty old, despite her attempts to maintain her youthfulness with a rather skimpy top of which I did not approve) or was being metaphorical. I decided to play the ignorance card.

"Oh, what's up there?" I tentatively asked, hoping the answer wouldn't be a large bag of sh*t balanced delicately above a fan.

"Nuthin', no buildings." Excellent. Sounds like quite the trip. I'll probably book it for Monday... I slipped off into the rain.

Last night I went for dinner with some of my 'dormies' (I'm sure that's the fashionable name for them) where we got a free meal when we bought a drink. Result! It was pretty small and basic (as expected) but nice. By now I was absolutely shattered, and so headed to bed shortly after, but not before I spoke to a girl I knew from university. Well I *had* been here twelve hours now, and it had to happen sooner or later.

Day 6

Yesterday was a bit of a write off because of Cyclone Hamish. In between trips out and getting soaked, a few of us went down to the bar and played cards.

The Americans taught me some games, I taught them some, and the Canadian guy taught us all that hurricanes rotate clock-wise and cyclones rotate anti-clockwise. Just like that water flushing business. Although I wasn't sure where that left an anti-cyclone...but I didn't want to ruin his moment. Whatever it is, it was a hemispherically educating afternoon.

In the evening a group of us went down to the bar for yet more card games, but this time with the addition of drink.

Now when it comes to downing pints, I'm often dangerously close to the 'little girl with pig-tails' category, but here, amongst Americans and girls (and girly-Americans) I shone. This was lucky as I kept having to do it, but I'm sure that nation will be proud as I fought to maintain the UK binge-drinking reputation.

It was a fun night (if a little hazy) despite 'someone' smacking their shin on a stage platform that *definitely* must have been moved there just as I...I mean 'someone' turned to walk off. Luckily it didn't affect my 'emotionality' too much.

Yes, I thought you would frown at that. I guess it must be a Canadian word...

Today is brighter. Perfect for a boat trip. *Sigh*.

I went down to the lagoon and read. You fly ten thousand miles to the other side of the globe to do something you could do in your room at home. Silly really. Although here I had the added inconvenience of a little girl splashing around me. I wished I'd had a ball I could throw so she could fetch it and bugger off. But then realised that that's probably not how you treat children, and why I'm best off not around them. So I left.

Little girl 1, Chris 0.

Day 9

On Sunday I finally got to scuba dive! It was a hot sunny day. We went to two locations, diving at the first and snorkelling at the second. We saw a lot of fish and coral stuff. I guess that's that barrier reef business. Tick! I also saw a stingray! Now you don't get those in the River Gade!

It was really good, and they put on a good array of food for lunch, which is always a bonus. I also got chatting to a guy who turned out to be an ex-flatmate of a friend in Southampton who I've probably met before. It really is a small world...or maybe we're all just unimaginative travellers.

I got up early on Monday for work...I mean to get the bus. My first Oz Experience...experience. It was lively. We stopped at a crocodile farm where we saw...you guessed it! Birds! But also crocodiles. We got to hold one too, *and* a python, and we fed wallabies and patted a dingo. It was farmtastic - better than those year two trips to the farm where the best you got to see was a cow sitting in a field and a diseased chicken.

We then carried on to Mission Beach where I'm staying in a very relaxed hostel - the complete opposite of Gilligan's in Cairns, which was party central in the town. Here you just lie about by the pool and play cards. I'm coping. My sandals broke yesterday though, so I had to stumble unfashionably into town to buy some 'thongs'. I've never been able to master the one strap design but I'm working on it.

Today I went down to the beach, but you still can't go in the sea as its jellyfish season. Why do they always book *their* holidays at the same time as mine? I'm thinking of changing travel agents.

Mission Beach is also home to one of Australia's infamous 'Big Things'. It is here you will find the Big Cassowary. A cassowary is essentially a big bird that can hurt you if you piss it off. We learnt that at the farm. Who said travelling couldn't be educational?

Day 11

As '5ive' rightly once proclaimed, you've got to "keep on movin'", and so yesterday (after a very cold night due to the over-compensating air-conditioning that caused me to have to hunt about in my bag for my silk sleeping bag liner, which I then struggled to get into, and then once I *was* in, got very tangled and only fell unconscious due to the over exertions of trying to free myself) I followed this solid piece of melodic advice and re-packed my boardies and boarded the bus to Townsville, home to Australia's six-finger discount. Well what would you expect from a town that I'm reasonably sure means 'townstown'? I'm sure our bus driver was an ambassador for the place too, as presumably is his wifesister...but he was nice enough all the same.

It was early evening by the time we arrived in the capital of North Queensland, having experienced numerous heavy downpours along the way. We then boarded the ferry for the half hour crossing to Magnetic Island*. It was a windy trip out on deck, followed by a bus from the main harbour to the hostel on the other side of the island. A ten-minute ride through the hills led us to Bungalow Bay YHA at Horseshoe Bay, a really tranquil set of hut-dorms surrounded by noisy wildlife.

This morning I went in the outside swimming pool before catching the bus with Josh (who I met at Mission Beach and we were on the same bus yesterday, and we're now staying at the same hostel on Magnetic Island) to the ferry terminal, where we walked along the beach, swung on some swings, and bought some food from the supermarket (having used the world's slowest cash machine, which I'm reasonably sure shipped the money in from the mainland during the transaction). This afternoon it was back to the pool. It's a tough life.

*Irrelevant fact: *Magnetic Island was so named after Captain Cook was sailing nearby, and his compass started "sh*tting about"* (that's the kind of descriptive quality you get from the Oz bus drivers) *so he got out his spare and that did the same. After extensive research and testing, the island was found to have no magnetic field or influence.*

Day 12

Today is significant. Today is Day 12. Today is Red Nose Day (for which I especially burnt my nose in preparation for). Today marks the longest time I've spent abroad in recent times without getting into difficulties, and today is Friday 13th. Today was also the day I chose as my first attempt at moped-ing. Today was nearly the day I got splattered on the front of a lorry whilst attempting my first attempt at moped-ing. Tomorrow shall be the day I take the bus.

I got up early, and went with Josh to hire some mopeds. After finally tracking down the hire place (a house - no signs, advertising or anything) we set off, and spent the day zipping across the island, stopping for a koala trek (in thirty-five degree heat up hills) and at various beaches and bays.

It was great fun, and on our road trip (similar to the Top Gear Vietnam Special in many ways) we saw some fantastic scenery and wildlife, and no people. Every beach is virtually (if not completely) deserted.

We were lucky enough to see a koala on our koala trek (otherwise god knows what we would have called it!) but only because a nice Australian lady pointed it out to us. It was right above our heads in a eucalyptus tree, and inevitably it was asleep, as apparently they sleep for up to twenty hours a day. Similar to some of the backpackers I've met actually...

It was perhaps this excitement and sense of freedom (and the massive engine power of the moped) that led me to approach a tight and steep bend around the coastal road at slightly too higher speed, just as a large lorry came around the upcoming corner. The front of the white lorry cab was a little plain and boring, but I still felt that it was a little too early in my trip to warrant sacrificing myself in order to decorate it with my organs. Luckily I managed to pull out of its path, and I even had eight or nine metres to spare! No sweat.

Despite this, Magnetic Island really is a great place to spend a few days, despite some people telling me before that it wasn't. These people need locking in the grimy Magaluf toilets where their travel dreams presumably exist.

Oh, and I forgot to add; I'm pretty sure that for those six mopederific hours we were the two coolest looking people in the world. Probably.

*Thong update: *After persistent thong wearing, I have upgraded my single-strap footwear competency level from 'nomadic stumbling' to 'flip-flop fluency'.*

Chapter 6

Grabbing Goats and Sailing Boats
Thoughts of a Sea-Faring Outback Adventurer

Day 13

I'm currently sitting in the ferry terminal at Townsville waiting for the bus. I just overheard some of the Aussie country kitchen style daytime television programme on the screen above.

"Nothing is as respectable as being completely English. And nothing is as English as afternoon tea."

What? Is this *really* the Australian view of us? A respectable nation of tea-sippers? I don't really know where to begin with the naive, cliché and out-dated issues with that. I think the wild binge drinking and associated behaviour of last night's full-moon party could have straightened a few misinformed Aussie daytime television watchers out though.

Despite the huge hype of last night's party, maybe predictably it was a disappointment. For a start it wasn't *even* a full moon! From mine and many others's perspective the draw was going to be the beach. The beach that we *weren't* allowed on.

Luckily the pre-party games with dorm buddies, Josh, Liberty, Nicky and the gang, and the care-free (and more than likely licence-free) bus driver made up for the ridiculously overpriced ASBO summer disco that followed.

It was largely expected though, especially having shared a dorm with some of England's finest. Arrogance vs. ignorance.

The spectacularly stupid and misguided snobs that you are sometimes forced to encounter abroad, can bring into question the challenges of travelling, possibly at the expense of travel-originality. On the plus side however, you do get classic quotes such as;

"Why would I do a boat ride here? I'll just go on my dad's speedboat back home if I want that."

Time for another glass of parent-funded champagne perhaps...

Day 15

Whitehaven Beach, Whitsunday Island. Not the worst place to spend your birthday.

Day 16

I've just got back from the Whitsundays sailing trip. The weather was excellent, the food was excellent, the water was excellent, and the beach was excellent. It was just all very excellent. There were eighteen of us on the boat, and us males were out-numbered fifteen to three. It was a good bunch of people though, which was just as well given the cramped conditions.

We sailed (...with the aid of a motor) to a cove on the first day where we snorkelled around and got fed. Then, with the wind in our...motor, we moved round to another bay where we ate again and spent the night.

There was a longer gap between feedings than I've just made out you'll understand, but I'm just being brief as when you're not snorkelling or eating you're just lazing about on the solid wooden deck feeling your rear-end get progressively more numb. They did feed us a lot though. Oh, and we were looking at the pleasant coastal surroundings some of the time too.

On the second day (having had 'happy birthday' sung to me in English, Norwegian, Swedish, German and er...Canadian, the previous night) we cruised round to a bay where we de-boarded the boat and trekked through to Whitehaven beach. Amazing.

For the first time in twenty-two years of seeing places, I had finally arrived at a location that looked as good as the photos. No wonder it is one of the top few beaches in the world, and the second most photographed sight in Australia. I'll let you guess which is number one.

So with a slightly renewed faith in holiday brochures, we spent a couple of hours casually strolling across the finest, whitest (and squeakiest! – apparently because it is 98% silica) sand I had ever seen, and splashed through the clear water as the sun shone, the breeze blew, and fish swam around our feet. It was quite surreal.

We then re-boarded the Freight Train (our boat) and had chicken, before sailing off to another bay for some more snorkelling.

In the evening (after our roast dinner) we ran out of fresh water for drinking. Just like they said *wouldn't* happen. We then went onto an island briefly, but decided the boat was better, so we went back on board and drank and played cards.

I'm now back in Airlie Beach and waiting to check into my hostel so I can shower, as my hair has developed a not hugely fashionable look thanks to the hair-moulding effects of three-days of sea water.

* * *

I'm now showered and doing laundry. Hopefully my clothes will finally be free of seawater and scuba-fins. I also just bumped into a guy who seems to be following me down the coast but three days behind. I also saw people I knew coming off the boat as I got on and I also just ran into Josh, my moped adventure buddy. I just saw a girl I recognised too, although I couldn't remember where the hell from so I let that one go. I can see this situation reoccurring more and more. I'm now going to meet a few of these fellow travellers at the lagoon.

Now I know it's St. Patrick's Day, but I'm sure that doesn't justify playing 'Fairytale of New York'. I've heard it four times in three days. They might be Irish, but it aint bloody New York. Or Christmas! They also keep playing 'Snow Patrol'. Erm, they're Northern Irish. United Kingdom? Never mind...

Sadly I won't get much chance to celebrate this Australian Christmas/UK St. Patrick's Day though, as I'm off early tomorrow on an eleven-hour bus journey to a cattle ranch to re-introduce myself to my cowboy roots. Wide-rimmed hats at the ready!

Day 17

Last night was lively. I was about to go out to get something to eat before meeting the boat trip crew for drinks, but then a few people came into the dorm and we ended up sitting around playing guitar.

Eventually I headed down and had some St. Patrick's Day themed green snakebite, and inhaled helium whilst impersonating Irish stereotypes. What more could you want from an evening?

During the evening I kept bumping into people I'd met from all up the coast. It's like being at university again (but warmer...and with more Canadians). I also got into a discussion with a little Scottish girl (she wasn't actually that small - I'm just trying to be patronising, but realise there is little point as she probably won't be reading this) who didn't believe it was cheaper to take the Oz bus south rather than north. She was very stubborn and argumentative, which only made it more satisfying when I realised we were in the hostel reception/travel agents, so I found the Oz brochure, opened it to the right page...then walked off into the night victorious.

Chris 1, Scotland 0.

I was up at half five this morning for the bus, and we're now speeding along to cowboy camp. Yeehar!

Day 18

Yup, we're back on the bus again, and this time heading for Hervey Bay.

After eleven hours of travelling we arrived at the cattle station in Kroombit early yesterday evening, but not before we had stopped off in a small town for a game of lawn bowls. As you do. Lawn bowls is a hugely popular sport in Australia, and this visit will only serve to increase the chances of it catching on back home and lowering the average age of participants. By about fifty. Maybe that's a bit harsh - I actually quite enjoyed it, although I find calling it a 'sport' just a *little* tenuous.

We checked into our wooden dorm cabins in the outback cattle station before eating a goat. Then we had roast beef. Can you spot the cattle ranch link? It's a toughie.

After dinner we got an 'outback talk' from an old man in a cowboy hat who then taught us how to whip a whip (and ourselves, inadvertently in the process). We were then challenged to ride a mechanical bull. Both were painful (albeit in different areas) but good fun.

After the pain had more or less subsided, we gathered into a circle and played some group games under the close scrutiny and instruction of a small German lady (who you would not want to argue with having heard her bark out orders) before heading to bed for a few hours sleep.

Sleep time was shortened by the very loud Canadian girls next door who kept flicking the lights on and off and repeatedly questioning each other about how drunk they were. They should have just asked me through the wall. I could *easily* have confirmed that they were indeed *very* drunk.

The only break from their excessive use of the word 'like' and irritating upward inflection came when they all spontaneously burst into a Celine Dion-esk, ear-bursting rendition of Queen's 'We Are The Champions'.

The next morning I overheard one of them asking one of the others;

"Were we singing last night?"

Yes. Yes you were.

* * *

Today I was up at six, had breakfast, and then boarded the bus to go for our ranching activities. We had a go at clay pigeon shooting (the first time for all of us) with a shotgun, and I hit the first two of my five orange pigeons. So watch out drunken Canadians!

We then took part in a rodeo, which I always associated with over-priced fairground rides and little children on candyfloss-induced sugar highs. Here it meant *literally* grabbing the goat by the horns (presumably a less decisive version of grabbing the bull by the horns) tipping it up, branding it, then dragging it into a pen - all in groups of four. The goats seemed to love it...

We were then all pulled together into a circle and group-tasered. Classic Oz hospitality.

After the buzzing died down most people went horse riding, but given my recent bad luck with being bitten by a horse shortly before coming travelling, I decided that quad biking would be the safer option. I was mistaken. It was pretty dangerous but hugely fun as we tore through the outback on the twenty kilometre off-road adventure, and we were all left with a stylish dust-tan and a few bruises for good measure.

It was then back on the bus to head out of the outback ranch and back into the outback before heading back out of the outback and back to the coast.

Oh, and it's raining.

Day 22

Nothing says Australia like a kangaroo. Which is ironic really, seeing as kangaroos can't speak, but apparently they can jump nine metres, and if they choose to do this across a road they can make an awful mess on your windscreen.

Our Oz Experience bus drivers are sometimes very knowledgeable, and give an often fascinating insight into this vast country. For example; around 98% of the population live on the East coast (21 million), which is only 2% of the land. Sadly 98% of the people on the buses are too tired or hung over to appreciate this.

* * *

Laundry. I'm currently waiting for all the sand and dingoes to be washed out of my clothes having arrived back from the 4x4 expedition around Fraser Island.

It was a very bumpy three days, but a lot of fun. It was also quite strange. Driving along a beach isn't something I do much of unless I take a seriously wrong turn (although it was the first place I drove when I was ten) but this time there were nine other people in the back, and instead of stopping at rocks/tree stumps/fishermen, you just drive over them.

My two nights in Hervey Bay prior to the trip were unusual because I had a dorm to myself for the first time on my travels. It was almost lonely. It was certainly colder. This was therefore a *big* contrast to being crammed into a tent with three people, or bouncing around in a group of ten in a 4x4.

The evening before we left for the world's largest sand island we had a briefing. This involved a series of forms where we had to sign our lives away, and a patronising safety video about how to stack a box.

After this was over we had to go group shopping. Somewhat inevitably, stupid purchases were made. The purchase of five hundred grams of table salt being a fine example. I mean, what the *hell* were we going to do with *five hundred grams* of table salt? Answer: Nothing. Other than spill it. Everywhere. Repeatedly. I have to assume it's these ridiculous Fraser Island groups that are responsible for the high salt content in seawater.

Luckily the huge amounts of bread that were bought (white, brown, wholemeal, camel-shaped, multigrain, seeded, - some people have bizarre priorities) were of more use, and having managed to talk them out of buying a bag of sugar (?!) we were set. Well almost. There was another painful and repetitive three-hour briefing first, *and* we had to endure a small fat man shouting incomprehensibly at us about spatulas. We didn't even *have* any spatulas.

A short drive down the road and a twenty-minute ferry crossing left us free on this vast island for three days of bouncing along dirt/sand tracks and beaches. It was brilliant, and *great* fun to drive on. There's still something strange about indicating on a beach though. Oh, and you had to be constantly aware of aeroplanes landing next to you. Just standard road stuff really.

Both nights we camped by the beach and cooked lots of meat, and of course we served this with everyone's favourite condiment - sand.

Last night (against all odds) I managed to cook pasta. And no, this *wasn't* me being useless, but because the stove didn't really work, and it was tough boiling water in the rough, windy terrain. In the end it was more out of principle. Especially as it tasted like...you guessed it! Sand. We also watched helplessly as a rogue dingo gate crashed our party and stole a loaf of bread. They're crafty little buggers.

We had been told of numerous conflicting methods for defending ourselves against the menace of these dog-fox animal things, from running away as fast as you can, to staring them in the eye and holding your ground. We were also told to cross our arms over our chest...possibly as some kind of biblical offering...but the best I recall was;

"You have to sing at them really loudly". I think they *may* have been taking the mick. It certainly made me look silly.

Both days we got to swim in amazingly clear, fresh water lakes. These both served as showers *and* entertainment. Two of us tried swimming across one of the lakes, but after an hour decided it was probably too far, and we were also unconvinced that we *weren't* being hunted by crocodiles.

Lake Wobby is a lake that's apparently cursed, and so aboriginals won't visit it. A group of rowdy backpacker's have slightly different beliefs however, and no one could deny the fun of sliding down the steep sand banks before diving into the rapidly diminishing (due to sand filling it up) catfish-filled lake.

Further on into our island adventure we encountered Lake Mackenzie. A world-renowned beauty spot, and it's easy to see why. The crystal clear water laps calmly onto the white sandy beach. You could happily splash about in the water and drink it, as it was so pure.

* * *

I'm now tired and hungry, and so my clothes better hurry up and dry. I'm also sporting some rather stylish eye-lines, presumably from my decision to not wear sunglasses and to squint instead. I'm sure these markings will be the height of fashion come the summer.

Day 23

I have arrived in Rainbow Beach. In twelve hours I shall leave Rainbow Beach.

Earlier today I had made a sort of half-arsed attempt at booking accommodation for tonight. I found an email address for a hostel someone had told me about, and after enquiring about room availability, I soon had a reply from someone called Erin saying they did have beds available, so I replied saying; "Great, see you tonight!".

What Erin had failed to tell me was that she wouldn't be there when I rode into town at the ridiculous hour of seven in the evening. That's right, 7.00pm! Even the bloody gate was locked! This place is a compulsory stop for Oz Experience bus travellers so I thought it might be a little more accommodating for the hundreds of people who presumably pile through here every month - where they *have* to stay the night.

Anyway, luckily someone was leaving through the gate and so they let me in, but there was no staff! Reception was locked up. The worst part now being that I was now locked *in*! In the end I had to ask one of the guests who obviously knew the narrow arrivals time policy to release me with her key. So screw you Erin! You just missed out on $22 and my impeccable reception manner!

I wandered down the road to the next hostel. This one featured an open gate system that was ideal for my entrancing needs. But the reception was closed on this one too!

Luckily I managed to find my way around to the bar, and after asking the barman if there was room for the night (I felt like Mary and Joseph at Christmas. Not both of them of course. I may have been confused by this place but I was still pretty sure I was only one person - one person in need of a bed) and luckily he came up trumps and sorted me out with one. He still seemed a little bewildered that I was keen to eat something at such a late hour (7.15 pm). This room didn't even have an Ox in it either, just a couple of girls who aren't especially forthcoming with pulsating conversation. Just thick Mancunian accents. I think I'll do some reading. The voice in my head reads without a Mancunian accent thankfully, although it is developing a hint of Irish...

* * *

When travelling you meet a lot of different people from a lot of different places. Actually that's a lie. One in three people you meet are from Reading. But of the foreign contingency, you start to recognise certain stereotypes that people tell you about.

For instance;

- The French are rude. Yesterday one talked too loudly near me. There was no need.
- The Swedish do *all* have blonde hair.
- American's rarely leave the U.S. and when they do, sometimes they're disliked. Apparently the ones that do escape the States sew Canadian flags onto their bags to avoid problems.
- The Canadians can't really seem to drink. "Like, oh my god! Like, that beer is, like, 4% alcohol!"

- The Irish can't seem to stop drinking. "Ya'man put a feckin' straw in me pint, so I punched him!"
- The Germans are hyper efficient. At camp on Fraser Island, the Essex contingency had a tent putting up competition* to see who was the quickest. Both groups were comfortably beaten by the German girls who weren't even competing.
- And then there's us Brits. Well, we're just a nation of tea-sippers at the height of sophistication and respectability…

How many Essex girls does it take to put up a tent?

Answer: *Three. Two to flap about and incorrectly assemble the frame, one to sit in the car and apply their make-up and fake-tan in the rear-view mirror, and a German to put it up properly, in between cooking and strategically investing in the Deustchebahn rail network.*

Day 24

I have arrived in Mooloolaba! It was a little unplanned admittedly. I was supposed to be in Noosa, but through a combination of having nowhere to stay and it being a place for rich people and high quality ice cream appreciators (of which I fit into neither category) I've wound up at the next stop down.

But, if I'm right in thinking a place should be judged by how many vowels it has in its name, it should be good. In fact with such a stunning vowel to consonant ratio, I've decided to stay for two nights (nothing to do with that coinciding with the next available bus of course).

Day 25

This morning I had toast on the Sunshine Coast. I also had Vegemite. I feel like such a traitor to my strong Marmite heritage.

Last night I got I.D.ed when I walked into an alcohol shop. They really are strict out here. I didn't even have time to *look* at any alcohol before the till girl (who was probably younger than me) struck. There are a few strange laws out here regarding alcohol, such as the law that means bars have to close for ten minutes every hour. All this achieves is creating a large queue, and inflicts sustained annoying drunken 'bar-talk' on the bar staff.

The reason I was getting some beers was because I've drunk very little since being away, and I was getting worried that I would be out of practice. It would also serve as a fine accompaniment to the all you can eat pizza that the hostel was putting on. I planned on using this as an opportunity to stock up my stomach for a few days. To be honest, even though they said 'all you can eat', I was still up for more after twelve slices when they ran out, but I suppose I got my $4 worth. I've decided not to sue, but if we were in America...

The eating mainly served as a social interaction opportunity. Ah, who am I kidding, I was there for the food, but I did get involved in a bottle-top flicking drinking game with some Brummies, and then after watching a pirate copy of 'Slumdog Millionaire' on the projector screen, we played cards until the early hours.

Today I got up and went jet skiing that I had booked yesterday. It was hugely fun bouncing over the surf at 70km/h, even getting 'air' and accidentally knocking over the instructor in the safety boat whilst navigating the shark infested waters. People who saw me probably thought I was some kind of crazy motorised pirate I imagine. I have a good imagination like that. The reality was that I probably looked like a power-crazed child let off his dungaree safety straps too early.

Anyway, that satisfied my 'new place – new activity' policy, so tomorrow it's off to Brisbane in search of more adventures...

Chapter 7

Tall Things and Big Wheels
Thoughts of an Israeli Pop Diva Enthusiast

A French man started chatting to me at breakfast this morning.

"So what do you think of the rooms? They're horrible don't you think? It's like being in prison."

No Comment...

Day 27

I got on the bus yesterday to find twelve people from the cattle ranch leg of the trip on board. It was like cowboy camp reunited! We arrived in Brisbane around two hours later, and after checking into our rooms a few of us went off for a wander around the city.

It felt really strange to be in a big city having spent the last month in lots of small beach resorts. I also appeared to have completely lost the ability to cross roads properly, and was nearly embedded into the clean Brisbane road network on numerous occasions.

We stopped for a Chinese meal on our wanders, and then I went off for some more exploring (including a bizarre chat with a woman who liked my shorts) before meeting back up with the others for some drinking games on the terrace, where vast quantities of 'goon' were consumed.

I realise that I have written extensively about my time in Australia, yet failed to mention the Oz backer's drinking phenomenon up to this point.

'Goon' masquerades as wine, and comes in a four litre, silver space-bag format. Backpackers swear by it, simply because it's cheap. It's cheap because every time you drink it, a part of your soul dies. On closer inspection of the box (not advised) you discover that it contains traces of milk and fish pieces. How this substance comes into contact with fish pieces in its production phase is a mystery probably best left unsolved. So, having consumed our body weight in gill and fin juice, we went off to a bar.

It was a pretty standard experience as far as going to a bar goes, and after a while some of the girls decided we should go to another place. Sadly this meant a taxi ride. Now I hate taxis. The idea of being driven around while you're forced to watch your hard(ish) earned pennies disappear at an alarming rate on a small LED screen positioned mockingly in front of you, when you could be out exploring on your own feet really gets to me. *Especially* when you arrive and the girls decide we should head straight back in the same direction to the original place. *Sigh*.

Taxi-dictators 1, Chris 0.

A little later (when we had wound up at a reasonably indifferent club) one of the guys couldn't get in as he didn't have the right sort of ID, so I took this opportunity to make a break for freedom...for adventure!

I asked a bouncer which way the station was (which was near our hostel) and he frowned, shook his head, and said, "It will take you at least half an hour." Whatever. *I* was mashed on fish guts! I was *sure* I could do it in less. So I set off excitedly into Australia's third largest city, a city I had only known for a few hours, and without a map, but with a head full of goon.

Twenty exciting minutes later, I was back at the hostel.

Chris 1, faithless Australian bouncer and the entire greed-driven taxi industry 0.

I woke up this morning with a headache. The goon you may suggest (and it would be a reasonable guess) but no. I have a pretty good tolerance to alcohol, but sadly I do not have such a good tolerance to repeatedly slamming my head against metal bed frames. Bottom-bunk syndrome strikes again.

Once I had fully regained consciousness I ventured out into the city once again. This time I headed for the South

Bank. It's very impressive. I had heard that Brisbane was boring and not worth visiting, but once again these misguided individuals (who no doubt spend their evenings enthusiastically propping up the taxi industry) have missed the point of travelling. To see places. Not just the bottom of glasses. So there. How grown up do *I* sound?

Brisbane is an incredibly clean, modern, and vibrant city (apparently it was the second fastest growing city in the world after Dubai) and what completed the enjoyable morning of exploration was the discovery of a big wheel!

You're probably now fully aware of my fascination with being voluntarily detained in isolated glass capsules suspended high in the air, and once again I was in my element. I happily swung about in the breeze while snapping away on my camera as I looked eagerly out across the Brisbane skyline. It was a wheely ferris-satisfying morning.

Day 28

I'm now in Surfers Paradise (or Surfers Parasite as I've heard some people call it) despite our bus breaking down, and therefore we had to be rescued by another bus to finish off the journey.

Before I left Brisbane this morning I went back to the South Bank. I had been there the night before to witness 'Earth Hour', where Brisbane and other cities around the world switch off power to lights for sixty minutes in order to save the world. Only a couple of lights seem to go out at eight thirty, so presumably the world is doomed, but it was still a nice view all the same.

Today I sat on the riverbank and listened to music and wandered around the Queensland Museum and Queensland Art Gallery to buff up on some Australian culture. To be honest it didn't take very long, but that was *probably* more down to my efficiency and the fact that a lot of the galleries were closed, and not because the Australian's are a little short on it.

* * *

In my brief visit to Rainbow Beach earlier this week, I lost a bit of faith, a fair amount of dignity, and *all* of my shower gel. I feel in retrospect that this may have been a subconsciously intentional offering to the gods of sanitation, to acknowledge the highest standard of dorm en-suite facilities I have experienced on this trip so far, but in reality it was just an irritating mistake. I now keep forgetting to replenish it, so hopefully by writing this I *will* remember.

Day 29

I forgot to get shower gel.

I got up today and walked over to Q1, Surfers Paradise's tall building. I bought a discounted ticket (thanks to a voucher book I found) and then climbed seventy-seven floors in forty-three seconds (Okay, so I took the lift) and then found myself at the top of the twentieth tallest building in the world! AND the world's tallest residential building apparently! I can practically hear your gasps and cries of envy. It did have some good views.

I then wanted to go surfing (the name of this place providing that fantastic suggestion) but the weather turned for the worst. Rain, rain, rain. Now this place really wasn't living up to its 'Paradise' name. Oh how I miss the temperate sunshine of a mild English Spring.

Day 30

I bumped into fellow Oz busers, Holly and James this afternoon, and as the weather was so rubbish we all went bowling. I then found out that Holly wanted to parasail. Success! I had tried to book this yesterday, but the lady on the desk said it was a tandem activity, and that I needed a friend. I told them I didn't *have* any friends. They just laughed.

But this morning, now armed with a friend, and after a night of alcohol induced wandering, we managed to track down the parasail 'centre'. It was a tent. Not even a proper tent. No sides, just a makeshift table and a woman inside. No wonder their location was hard to pinpoint on the map at the hotel reception, it probably changes every day as they forget where they last put it up! It also happened to be right by the deserted broken down Oz Experience bus that we had to abandon the previous day.

Parasailing was really good. We got dragged along the water and blown high into the air, all whilst keeping an eye out for sharks. There was even a Japanese lady there who lived up to their tourist stereotype and was pretty handy with the camera. We spent half an hour being blown about above the waters of the Gold Coast, which was now conveniently basking in glorious sunshine.

Once back ashore we found a bus to take us back to Surfers Parrot Slice, and then we had to pack up and prepare for the trip to the next destination - Byron Bay.

I still have no shower gel.

Day 31

Time can get confusing. Last weekend British Summer Time kicked in. Yesterday we crossed from Queensland into New South Wales, but despite not making any eastwardly longitudinal advances, we still had apparently crossed a time zone, so we had to put our clocks forward one hour. Then on Sunday, Australia, or just New South Wales...I don't know, entered Daylight Saving Time, so the clocks went back again. I'm *reasonably* sure it's Wednesday though.

We therefore arrived in Byron Bay at a wide selection of times, but mostly it was evening. My hostel is only three weeks old, and as a result it is very clean, modern, and strangely 'spacey'. Sadly the prices are also in accordance with this theme of being out of this world. I had no other option though, as everywhere else had been booked up.

I met Holly and James for drinks and card games before heading to bed reasonably early, as I had agreed to go with *other* Oz busers, Jess, Kelly and Jack to see the sunrise at Australia's most easterly point.

I got approximately no sleep at all, so when it struck ridiculous o'clock (4am) I was raring to go. It took over an hour of trekking in the dark, slipping on the wet paths and rocks in our inappropriate footwear (and thongs!) before we arrived at Cape Byron. The waves smashed ferociously against the rocks below, and the sunrise was...well, a little slow and drawn out to be honest, but suitably dramatic to make it a worthwhile trip. We even saw a shooting star! We then all took a photo by the sign to prove we had been there, and then took a walk around the nearby lighthouse before returning to the town.

When I got back I had to hang around while I exchanged numerous confusing phone calls from a guy named Steve who I had booked to go hang gliding with yesterday. I booked it yesterday that is, I hadn't booked to *go* yesterday, that would have been careless. I wasn't *that* messed up by all the time changes.

After a lot of hanging about (not in the air) I was delivered...back up to the lighthouse where I had been this morning. I was then strapped into a sleeping bag and asked to sign my life away for the hundredth time this trip, before running and jumping off the skyward platform. It was brilliant.

We soared around over the hills and the Pacific Ocean for around half an hour, like a giant double-headed seagull (alright, metaphors aren't my strong point) while I carefully failed to take any decent photos with my one available hand. People watched on from below as we circled the headland at Cape Byron. Steve then shouted to me over the wind, "make sure you stand up when I tell you during landing – otherwise the cross bar will break your neck". I can see why he didn't mention this before take-off.

We then took one last swoop over a dolphin colony before making a dramatic and speedy landing on the narrow strip of beach (necks thankfully intact) allowing just enough time to get behind the neighbouring sand dunes before the waves dragged us out to sea.

I then returned to Byron Bay in search of more adrenalin buzzes, and so I ran into the sea to get battered by the most powerful waves and currents I have ever experienced. Hopefully I'll get some sleep tonight.

Oh, and I finally bought some shower gel.

Day 33

I'm in Sydney! After a month of backpackering I have successfully navigated my way around the most popular backpacker stretch of Australia. This isn't quite the solo achievement that it might be though, as with the package holiday styling's of Oz Experience there is little room to mess up. They can test you though, as I experienced when I turned up to the main bus stop in Byron (after another night of minimal sleep) half an hour early.

Ten minutes late, the Oz bus drove past. Five minutes later I phoned one of my bus buddies who said the driver ("Muppet" - fitting...) was going to go off without me, as I hadn't shown up. Luckily they told him where I was...at the *main pick-up point...* and soon I was picked up, and once I had completed the walk of shame past every other full seat on the bus, we headed to surf camp.

There seems to be a quota for Oz bus drivers regarding the number of swear words they must get through during each journey, and "Muppet" certainly didn't want to let the company down.

"Are you gonna throw up?!" (Grinning wildly.) "That's fuckin' sic! I love it! It makes me fuckin' happy!"

Lovely chap.

We arrived three hours later at surf camp, where we were greeted by the most cliché Aussie 'surf dudes' you could imagine. We dumped our stuff and then had our surf lesson briefing. It wasn't so much about how to surf, more about how to look cool whilst holding a surfboard. From what I can work out, this is achieved by wearing sunglasses when it's cloudy.

Eventually we hit the beach, and here we went through the basics of surfing; Lie on board. Stand up on board. Do not fall off board. Simple. And with this in mind, we ran off into the sea (of *course* we didn't! We strutted casually down the beach, winking at girls as per instruction) and then we were all soon 'wiping out' on some of the most storm-enhanced, shark-filled waves in Australia. It was awesome.

After two hours of being battered by waves, surfboards, and fellow surfers, we emerged from the sea, bruised, tired, and hungry, but very happy. We then showered and had a much-appreciated meal, and then we sat around a fire before agreeing we had passed the threshold of dignity for an early retirement (9pm) and went to bed.

Today was an early start for the nine-hour bus journey to Sydney, which concluded with a dramatic drive across Sydney Harbour Bridge. It was all very exciting, and after a forty-five minute trek through the city during rush hour, and with all my bags and wearing thongs, I eventually found my hostel.

I'm now about to play cards with some Swedes, although I'm not convinced they *are* Swedish, because they all have dark hair. The Canadians aren't disappointing their stereotype though...

What do you get if you combine eight Canadians with half a cup of goon?

NOISE! SO MUCH NOISE!!

I've also importantly just noticed that the twenty-four hour reception has now closed.

Day 34

Today has been fun. I actually got a decent night's sleep and so I was up and raring to go at nine o'clock. I had arranged to meet up with my mum's, friend's, husband's, brother (because that's what you do when you travel...) called David, and he phoned to say himself and Tim would pick me up from my hostel in Woolloomooloo (vowel: consonant ratio sending this place through the ratings roof!) and then they took me off over the harbour bridge to various bays around the world's largest natural harbour.

It was really nice to have a break from the backpackering lifestyle for a few hours, and it was also good to get some local insight into this world renowned city from a couple of its residents.

After they very kindly treated me to lunch, they dropped me back in the city mid-afternoon and I began to wander about as I have become accustomed to. I headed through Hyde Park and the Botanic Gardens to the Opera House. The view of this icon of Australia, framed by its neighbouring attraction - the harbour bridge, was certainly impressive, and so I did what everyone else was doing. I got in the way of everyone else's photos as I took my own.

Despite being opened by the Queen in 1973 (oh yes, I've done my research!) it still looks very clean and modern (admittedly it may have had the odd dusting and lick of paint in that time) and when it catches the sunlight it is truly an impressive sight from any angle. I then felt a sudden surge of frustration that I had come all this way to see one of the world's most recognised buildings, and yet I hadn't been inside. So I went into the Opera House foyer, and there things took an exciting twist.

You can pay to go on a tour of the building, but this seemed a little too touristy for me – the tourist, so I had a look to see what was on in terms of performances. I had no idea if this was a stupid quest as things may book up ages in advance, but I figured it was worth a shot. There was a comedy show on, but after irritating the receptionist with my bizarre line of questioning I discovered that this was taking place under the Opera House. I didn't want to be *under* it, I wanted to be *in* it. In the main concert hall ideally. She gave me a 'What's on' guide (presumably to disperse me from her company) and after assessing it, I returned to a different ticket office lady, who was far more entertained by my strange requests.

"Hello!" I opened cheerfully. "I'd like to go into the Opera House please. I don't care what I see; I just want to be inside. I'll even sit behind a pillar if I can get it at a reasonable price."

And as a result she was much more forthcoming with useful information. Anyway, to drag out a reasonably short story, I purchased a ticket to see 'Rita'.

Now, sometimes I lie awake at night dreaming of being in a fairly distant row...and slightly to the left [stage right] watching an Israeli pop diva. Tomorrow my dream will come true.

It was perfect. It was being held in the main concert hall, at a reasonable time (I have a strict bedtime you see...) AND it's her Australian debut! What more could you ask for? I even possess a slightly worrying amount of knowledge of Israeli pop divas thanks to my extensive studies on the Eurovision Song Contest for my university dissertation. This came in handy immediately in fact, as the lady offered me a bargain ticket for the front area for a mere $149. Now I'm aware due to my studies that most Israeli pop divas are clinically obese transvestites who wear ridiculously elaborate make-up and outfits, and so I graciously declined, and opted for a more distant viewing area for far more backpacker-friendly $39. Perfect. I can't wait!

I skipped out of the Opera House, beaming (now I obviously didn't skip - I'm not *that* sad) eagerly clutching my Israeli pop diva ticket. I meandered through circular harbour, crashing countless weddings along the way.

Earlier I had walked through a posh wedding at a smart country house on the way to a beach, and here I was walking through a wedding photo session of a Korean couple (they're big out here...no, not in size - they're still quite short, I mean in terms of numbers) who appeared to have just been wed in a steak house. Classy. I hope they got a free meal. I also saw another wedding party later on too. I think Israeli pop diva fever has definitely hit Sydney, and put love in the air.

I found a supermarket on my wanders, and here I purchased a hot lasagne for $3! And they said this city was expensive! I also bought a spoon. Actually I bought a soup spoon. Okay, okay, I bought six soupspoons for $1. They didn't sell forks or regular spoons, and I didn't fancy forking out (excuse the pun) for the hostel's cutlery set. This also meant that I was now perfectly set should five more well priced lasagnes present themselves over the coming weeks.

On my way back to the hostel I passed Marine Place. Apparently this is the place where you go to protest about things. I briefly stopped and requested Rita to be allowed to perform more dates in Australia, so that I could follow her on her great southern-hemispheric quest for stardom. I guess they'll get back to me...

I have now successfully soupspoon fed myself the lasagne, and so I now have five spoons left. All that remains now is for me to go to bed so that I can get a good night's sleep before tomorrow's excitements!

In fact in light of today's developments I may even forgive the fact that I'm staying in a hostel that is close to the drug/prostitute area of the city, in a room where the blinds don't work, where the 'fan' shakes the light to the noisy point of destruction, and where there is what appears to be a blood stain at the end of my bed. I'm also fairly certain that the man at reception has murdered members of his family. Ah well, I'm sure it will all be fine in the morning. Hopefully. If I'm still here.

Chapter 8

Travelling with a Soup Spoon
Thoughts of an Undiscovered Roulette Champion

Day 36

Yesterday morning (having thankfully survived the night) I went up Sydney Tower for panoramic views across the city. It was good to be high again. My decent proved a little tricky though, as they don't have very effective signage around here and I somehow ended up in the lingerie section of a top-end department store.

I had a brief paranoid flashback to when I was eight years old and used to get lost in BHS, and I would be found ten minutes later cowering under the maternity sleepwear racks sucking my thumb.

Luckily I am a little wiser now, and managed to navigate my way out without too much hassle. The only real issue that arose was when a woman offered me some 'Joop'. This sounded like something that the strange men on the streets near my hostel would offer me to smoke, but apparently its aftershave. I declined anyway, and was soon free of corporate Australia.

It's been a busy few weeks, and I think a month of travelling has finally caught up with me. My already rapidly diminishing concept of time peaked yesterday evening, when I arrived at Sydney's Ice Bar and was offered a six o'clock entry slot. As it was six thirty-five I felt that this might be pushing it a bit, even with my travel-efficient strategy.

Yup, I had forgotten to put my watch back an hour for daylight saving time.

Time 1, Chris 0.

I also have to keep trudging down the two floors to reception as my electronic swipe key keeps rejecting me entry to my room. When it happened this morning (for the fifth time in three days) I went back up three floors. No wonder I couldn't get in. And to top it all off I got trapped in the shower cubicle this morning as the lock mechanism broke when I was trying to facilitate my exit. I think I need a holiday.

I spent my thirty minute allocation in the minus five degree Ice Bar chatting to the barman as we were the only two in there. I had first noticed this novelty drinking establishment as I made my way back through the city after my successful visit to the Opera House ticket office the previous day, and had decided that this would be the perfect warm-up (again, excuse the ironic pun) for that night's festivities. There had been a group of very drunk, hair-product-endorsed Australians in there, who had initially thought I was going to

104

ask them to leave (presumably due to my authoritative appearance leading them to believe I worked there) so I did. I think they sussed me though, and then they found it funny. I didn't. Just get out. Soon after, they did.

Anyway, after drinking my free 'mocktail' from an ice cube that I grasped between two giant finger-impairing gloves, I left the Ice Bar. Due to my earlier time mess-up I was still quite early, so I sat on a bench outside the Opera House watching the twinkling lights of the city, before the hour arrived for my date with Rita.

The inside of the main concert hall is very impressive, and my front row aisle seat in the upper tier was perfect in the event I needed a quick escape. The highly polished laminate wood, combined with the plush red seating gave a thoroughly royal feel to the hall, and with the architectural complexities of the 'shell' design, it was undoubtedly a dramatic setting for what would be a fascinating evening.

First on was a string-based ensemble, whose eastern polyrhythmic sounds were wildly captivating. The acoustics of the venue allowed the virtuosic melodies to resonate dramatically around the hall, creating a mesmerising intensity to proceedings. Sadly they were only on for half an hour, and then there was an interval, where most of the occupied seats were vacated as people rushed off for refreshments. These people have no endurance. They've obviously never sat through a Lord of the Rings film.

Shortly before eight o'clock, Rita and her backing band came on to the stage to rapturous applause. It was then that I realised that the entire Israeli population of Australia had turned out to see her Aussie debut. Luckily I am a man of the world, and so by frantically clapping and imitating complimentary throat sounds, I fitted in seamlessly. Like a frostbitten hand into a size-adjusted, fleece-lined ski glove.

My only regret was that I had stupidly taught myself Mandarin on the flight to Singapore and not Hebrew. If only they had warned me that Rita was synchronising her visit with mine.

Now it has got to be said that Hebrew is not the smoothest of languages to sing in, and the overpowering vocal balance was often filled with the sound of a throat filling with saliva. Having said this though, I do owe Rita an apology. I had callously grouped her with my previous experiences of Israeli pop divas, but she certainly wasn't obese, and nor was she a transvestite.

This helped relieve me from the fear that had suddenly gripped me last night, that I, a lone male, was about to go and see a transsexual pop diva in the gay capital of the world. My carefully selected baggy clothing was therefore surplus to requirements. In fact to be very straight and English about her, at forty-seven years old - she scrubbed up alright for an old bird.

I had been right about one thing though, she did have Europop credentials, and so I would like to belatedly congratulate her on coming eighteenth in the 1990 Eurovision Song Contest.

It was altogether a thoroughly enjoyable evening, and certainly very different. After half expecting to find the need to make use of my close proximity to the exit, I ended up staying for the whole concert. I was very glad I did too, as who could have predicted the emotive power of the on stage finale that saw Rita team up with her daughter for a surprise duet.

It was also great to hear some live music again, even if half of it was from the man next to me, who, even after an hour and a half, still seemingly failed to develop any grasp of melody or timing.

Day 37

Yesterday was reasonably uneventful after the previous night's entertainment. In fact I think I had a bit of a Europop hangover, so I had a lie in until the crazy hour of 10am.

I then took a walk around the city (which was rapidly seeming like home, as four days is the longest I've spent anywhere on this trip) and I slipped into my only real routine of going to an underground supermarket* where I bought some bread 'n' stuff, then took it to a relatively secluded part of the botanic gardens that overlooks the Opera House and the harbour bridge, before dancing around it and chanting in Hebrew.

Okay, I ate it. I've already admitted to not knowing a lot of Hebrew - I was just trying to liven up a pretty dull event.

After lunch I walked through 'The Rocks' (the older part of the city) and then onto the harbour bridge. I chose not to pay the $250 or whatever it is to climb the bridge, and instead walked across it for slightly cheaper price of nothing.

By 'underground supermarket', I mean literally 'under the ground', and not some fashionable 'alternative' supermarket frequented by 'those in the know' or serving those with a very trendy or selective taste. It's actually called 'Coles', and I think it's a big chain.

Today was a little more exciting. I was going to meet my bus buddies, James and Holly and a few others to go to Bondi Beach, but after getting up at seven and checking the buses I found that they were walking to a far away bus stop in the opposite direction, so without any maps or directions, I set off walking in the direction I thought Bondi was.

I had been told that you needed to get a confusing itinerary of buses and trains to get there, but I was pretty sure it was more or less a straight line, and sure enough (despite a few forced detours through suburban Sydney) I arrived on Bondi Beach an hour and a half later.

I met the others and then spent a grand total of six minutes on the beach. I stuck my feet in the sea (actually it came up to my waste - I still haven't mastered the powerful waves yet) then, now with wet underwear, we wandered around the beachfront for a while and some of the others bought some cake.

We then headed back to the city on the bus, where they went off to climb the Sydney Tower (that was *so* yesterday!) while I went back to the ferry terminal to catch a ferry to Manly.

The water was quite choppy, but after a twenty-minute ride we moored up in the home of Australia's second favourite soap. It was nice. I *even* stayed for half an hour before catching the next ferry back. Sydney – done!

On my way back to my hostel from the ferry terminal I noticed lots of lighting rigs being set up, and red carpets being laid out in front of the Opera House. I decided not to hang around, as it was for the 'Star Trek' world premiere that was taking place that evening. I'm pretty sure there's already been a film called 'Star Trek' anyway. Maybe it was a case of 'Spock the difference'. Sorry.

Day 38

Today was an early start to begin the three day trip to Melbourne - Australia's nicest city*. Our first stop was in the ACT (Australian Capital Territory) and funnily enough, the capital of Australia - Canberra.

The first look at the city we got was from the top of Mount Ainsley, a mountain with a viewpoint that looks straight down the centre of the city and up to Parliament House.

We then wound our way down from the mountain and into the city, where on our way to the Government HQ we drove along a road that had all the different nation's embassies on. We played 'guess the flag' as they appeared one after the other on either side of the road until we arrived at Parliament House.

It was incredibly open and relaxed in terms of security. For instance, we parked right underneath where they decide all of Australia's laws. There was even an ATM inside! We got to sit in the Senate House (the only room in Australia to have red 'exit' signs) and the lower house (the House of Lords and House of Commons equivalent).

Our bus driver served as our tour guide and was incredibly knowledgeable and made it all very interesting. I think the reason that Australian history appeals is because so much of it is so recent. He also told us about some of the numerous scandals that had gone on in Australian politics, and how some of the country's leaders weren't *quite* as clean-cut as they would have liked to make out.

According to lots of people. Except for maybe Perth. That's also supposed to be quite nice.

* * *

We're now in Thredbo, an alpine ski resort in the Great Dividing Range. It really is a change from all the beaches of the east coast. There is something else that feels strange about this place…I *think* it's something I wouldn't associate with this country – being cold!

Day 39

Disaster has struck. Shower gel *everywhere*. That same bloody shower gel that I spent so long carefully forgetting to buy. I never did trust it, that's why I wrapped it in a bag and put it in the hood of my rucksack. Sadly I also decided to put my book and journal in there while I climbed Mt Kosciuszko, Australia's highest mountain.

I'm now tired and my journal smells like a well-groomed male. Sadly I don't, so I may have a shower…but I don't have any shower gel…and so you see the predicament I'm in. So basically, once *again* I need to buy some shower gel…

It was a really good fourteen-kilometre trek up to the top of Mt Kosciuszko. We took a ski lift up from Thredbo, and then set off on the rocky pathways. It was again not very Australian - more Scottish, except with more blue sky and sunshine then I recall Scotland ever having. It was perfect walking temperature, and with the vast, barren mountainous landscape stretching off as far as the eye could see, we trod happily along the stony paths. Once at the top we stopped for photographs, and some even called home to mark their achievement. Sadly these people still hadn't mastered the time difference between Australia and the UK, and so were a little confused as to why those on the other end of the phone weren't more impressed at their feat, or grateful for being told about it at 2am.

Other than the mountain trek it was a lot of time on the bus, with the occasional stop for wombats and rocks that *looked* like wombats. It was late evening by the time we arrived at Lakes Entrance*, which to be honest, I have no idea where it is. We did get fed though, and after a busy day we were all very hungry, and proceeded to eat our fish and chip dinner like a group of starved orphans.

Someone then passed around a slip of paper for everyone to write their names and email addresses on. I was about to write mine when I noticed the name above was 'Ambrose'. Creepy. I've never met another Ambrose out in the wild before. She's Australian, which means we probably share a great, great, great, great grand something...except her's probably stole a loaf of bread, and mine didn't. I won't hold it against her though. I'm nice like that.

* * *

I don't think Australia's predominantly dry landscape has rubbed off on their sense of humour. I regularly seem to end up in a hole (metaphorically I mean) when talking to them.

Bus driver: "Morning, morning, morning!"

Chris: "Morning! Shame about the weather!" (Clear blue skies and bright sunshine.)

Bus driver: "Oh, I thought it was pretty good."

Chris: "Er...yes, actually you're probably right..."

Lots of places and things in Australia are very simply or obviously named;

Great Barrier Reef - big reef, which acts as a barrier

Great Ocean Road - long road by the ocean

The Great Divide - big mountains that divide one side from the other

Blue Mountains - mountains that appear blue (supposedly)

The Outback - out back

The Bush – bushes

75 Mile Beach - a beach, seventy-five miles long

90 Mile Beach - a beach, ninety miles long

5 Mile Beach - well...you get the idea

Townsville – townstown

Lakes Entrance - entrance to the lakes

Sydney Tower - tower in Sydney

Sydney Harbour Bridge - bridge in Sydney harbour

Sydney Opera House - house in Sydney for Opera

Woolloomooloo - er...probably aboriginal for 'grubby underground car park that is

frequented by drug addicts and prostitutes'

Day 42

It's Easter Sunday (according to a newspaper headline I just noticed) and I'm sitting in Melbourne's Botanic Gardens under hot clear blue skies. Except for the plane that's just flown over and written 'Call Mum' in smoke in the sky. That was an expensive advert. And a bit pointless, I actually phoned her yesterday.

Easter is more of an inconvenience than anything else as it means there is less to do as places are closed, although it does mean a discounted tram ticket, which is a nice bonus.

We arrived in Melbourne two nights ago, and after wandering around in the dark, I finally found numerous sex shops. *And then* more importantly (and more intentionally) I found my hostel. I think that HostelWorld.com must be mainly used by drug addicts and prostitute users, as I *always* seem to end up in the hostels in areas where these are the predominant activities, and they always seem to have high review ratings for location.

The hostel is also called 'St. Kilda Beach House'. Now call me a crazed fantasist, but judging by the name I was hoping for a sort of…beachy feel to it. But other than it being in St. Kilda, the name has proven to be a little misleading. Instead of a light, bright summery feel that you may expect, it is a very dimly lit place, with bare breezeblock walls, metal rafters, corrugated steel ceilings, and grates and wires everywhere. I would argue that it is the perfect definition of a warehouse. The bathrooms are very flash and spacious though. Actually I may sleep in there, as the mattresses on the beds are plastic crash mats that you stick to when it is hot and are very noisy.

Yesterday I got up and met two of my bus buddies, Alex and Katherina, and we went off on a tram to take a look around the city. I went up another tall building – Eureka Tower (this one was *also* claiming to be the tallest residential building in the world, as QI in Surfers Paradise was) and then I took a walk around Melbourne Park - home to the Australian Open tennis.

We then met up again an hour later outside the Melbourne Cricket Ground to try and get some tickets for the evenings Aussie Rules match. I eventually tracked down an attendant inside one of the foyers of the massive 100,000-seater stadium, and after enquiring about tickets (as there were no signs) he just laughed in my face and asked if I was serious. I was. I didn't get him. Anyway I went around to another window and found a lady who found it a far less amusing request, and soon we had our tickets.

In the evening we went out for a Chinese meal in the city centre before making our way to the MCG. It was nearly full inside, and an incredibly lively atmosphere with all the fans of the two teams - Carlton and Essendon - all mixed up together. We just cheered when anyone else did, which confused others of our allegiances. Our seats were in the top tier, but we could still just about make out the ball, and eagerly watched the seventeen players on each side (plus *seven* referees!) run around the circular pitch kicking and throwing the ball whilst a couple of men in luminous yellow ran on and off the pitch collecting and delivering players. As you can tell, I am a massive and knowledgeable follower of AFL.

It was a really entertaining affair though, and after around two hours it ended in a dramatic 116 – 114 win for...er...one of the teams. *Possibly* the blue one.

Today I went to Albert Park where the Australian Grand Prix was held two weeks ago. I spent an hour walking around the track where they were still disassembling the stands and advertising hoardings. You might find it surprising how contented I can be following faded white lines around some tarmac, but it was an important activity to tick off my list.

It was then time to complete another, arguably far more important task, so I headed back to St. Kilda and met up with Katherina. As it was Easter we thought we should have an Easter egg. We set off to find some, but after a lot of searching we only managed to find some very small melted less-than-egg-shaped eggs in a petrol station. We bought them anyway though, and ate them on our way to the beach.

Once we got to the beach we had an ice cream to compensate for the rubbishness of the eggs. And yes I'm still forgetting to buy shower gel.

Day 44

The tram rides into the city over past couple of days have been entertaining, with today's driver remarking; "The major stops are announced, but please ring the bell to get off as the driver's function for reading minds is not working this afternoon." This was a nice informal approach to public announcements, which was only surpassed by last night's tram driver, who gave us a spontaneous rendition of 'Wonderful Tonight' as we made our way through the bustling city streets. He got a well-deserved clap at the end.

Yesterday I went up another tall building, but I couldn't go around the big wheel because the summer heat wave broke it. Stupid hot sun. They don't have it easy with all the droughts, fires or flooding they have in this country.

At the top of the tall building (once the second tallest building in the Southern Hemisphere!) I noticed that they were selling postcards (Note to self: I should probably send some sometime...) with one showing all the 'common' Aussie phrases, such as 'G'day', 'How you going?' and 'Camping with gas'.

What? When is that said?! Surely that's just something the more superior camper does? I don't get it. And I've *certainly* never heard it said.

I opened the door to my dorm last night into an Irish guy. It wasn't clear why he was standing right behind the door, but he was pretty drunk, and soon borderline-harassing a Yorkshire girl.

He asked me who I supported, and presuming he wasn't referring to a 'whose drunk and unstable' arm grabbing competition between the two of them, I answered in football terms. He seemed devastated that I wasn't a Manchester United fan, and then proceeded to fall to his knees and conduct a bizarre ritual of praise to the higher powers for Leeds United's recent descent through the football leagues.

None of this made a lot of sense (especially given his nationality) but I decided getting into a heated discussion of misguided football alliances with an angry drunk Irish potential sex-offender could only result in a delayed dinner, and I just wasn't prepared to let that happen.

During the night the Irish football cult leader turned up in our dorm. He was noisy and kept shining a torch everywhere. It wasn't even his dorm! He also touched my neck at one point (presumably looking for a spare bed...or a Leeds United fan to sacrifice to the gods of ridiculous reasoning) and tried creeping off…as if I wouldn't suspect him!.

I had to get up at five in the morning for my bus, and as I quietly crept out of the dorm having packed up silently in the pitch black, I think I accidentally trod on his badly placed mobile phone as it charged in the middle of the floor. Revenge is sweet. I've probably saved a few northern girls from stalker court proceedings too...

* * *

I'm now in Alice (Alice? Where the f*ck is Alice?! Northern Territories) Springs, and it's *very* hot again. There are also a lot of flies that you find yourself constantly batting away.

The flight here was interesting. I had a feeling we were going back into a ridiculous half hour time zone which I had first experienced passing through Darwin (which is also in Northern Territories) but was expecting the flight captain to confirm it anyway.

"Welcome to Alice Springs, where the time is...probably quarter to one." The cabin assistant announced to us over the tannoy.

Right. Thanks for clearing that up. I think this was probably the same lady who took my boarding pass as I made my way onto the plane and said "Row F." Yes. I had also read that. In fact I had read the full '12F', but maybe she couldn't manage all that carefully coded information as she was carrying a child in her arms. I'm not sure if she had stolen it or whether it was 'bring your children to work' day. Either way, it didn't result in me getting any free peanuts.

Day 48

It was a seven-hour bus journey from Alice Springs to Uluru (Ayers Rock) but we finally arrived at camp mid afternoon and cooked a barbeque lunch.

We then visited Kata Tjuta (The Olgas) and walked between the massive red rocks that jut dramatically out of the ground.

In the evening we drove to Uluru for the sunset. There were a huge number of tour groups at the viewing area, and some had table-clothed tables and champagne, while we had...sand in our shoes. I think they pay more. Whatever your social standing and resultant tour comfort levels, it was still cloudy for everyone. Nice rock though. If a little dusty.

On the way back we tried creeping onto one of the higher quality coaches, but it was dark, and so we accidentally ended up getting back onto our own cramped little bus, and soon we were back at camp and cooking a stir-fry.

That night we slept in 'swags' (canvas bags that you lie in under the stars/clouds/pounding rain) that were surprisingly comfortable. Much better than the sticky crash mats of the Melbourne hostel anyway.

It was a strange sensation being battered by the wind and rain, as well as getting sand blown in your mouth as you lie there, but at least it was dry rain*.

A tumbleweed attacked our camp soon after everyone had turned in for the night (I thought they only existed in cartoons or low-budget comedies) and it rolled through our gathering of swags, leaving a couple of people covered in sharp twigs. It was pretty funny really, but then I didn't have to spend the next ten minutes picking twigs out of my clothes.

Shortly after this incident there was a loud Canadian scream of "Snake!"

"Shut up and go back to bed" were the muffled groans of most of the group as we were just drifting off, but after a lot of kafuffle it turned out that a metre long Western Brown snake *had* crept into her swag.

Apparently this is the second most venomous snake in the world. A camping first for everyone, *including* all the guides, and it quickly became the big story around the campsite. Safe to say she didn't sleep in a swag again.

Dry Rain: Rain that falls but when you pat your head it feels dry. Simple.

The next morning we got up at five to see the sunrise at Uluru. It was pretty much like the sunset...only it ended lighter. There were still lots of clouds though.

We walked around the base which is roughly 6.5km, and then had a culture talk/walk led by our tour guide, who told us about how lizards used to shoot arrows at snakes that were bad, and this caused the dents in the rock, or something... As you can tell, I haven't completely grasped the aboriginal 'dreamtime' stories.

We also got to read the 'Sorry Book' in the tourist centre, in which people from all over the world (mainly Canada) have sent back bits of rock they took from Uluru as a result of bad experiences. One included a list of bad things that had happened to a man as a result of this, and it ended with;

"Then in February I had my second stroke, and as a result I died twice."

How unlucky is that?! No wonder he returned the rocks he took. But what bothered me most was that I couldn't see a 'no regrets' book, where people had profited from sacred Uluru rock possession.

We then set off on the four-hour drive to Kings Canyon, where we set up an exciting illegal fire. It was a really good outback night of fire-stories (stories told around the fire – not stories about fires) games and copious amounts of spaghetti bolognaise. I also learnt something invaluable, courtesy of Viktor the Swedish postman. Apparently there are two Swedish words that we use in the English language; smorgasbord (which I rightly or wrongly always associate with cheese) and ombudsman. You've got to love the facts you learn on your travels.

The next morning was another five o'clock start for a 10km scramble over the Kings Canyon rocks. This was arguably more dramatic than Uluru, but ssshh! I'll get in trouble with the tourist board if that gets out.

It was then back on the bus for the six-hour return trip to Alice Springs.

We got back from the three-day expedition very tired and pretty fed-up of the bus.

In the evening, having showered off all the red dust and snakes from our clothes and bodies, we met up for a meal.

It was an enjoyable evening, although we were all pretty shattered having spent about twenty-three hours on the bus in three days, and so it wasn't that late before everyone started heading back to their hostels for a slightly less weather-dependant sleep. I think I've spent over four days on buses in my seven weeks in Oz, and so I think that should guarantee me a loyalty bus pass for when I'm older.

The following afternoon's flight back from Alice Springs to Melbourne was as interesting (or worrying) as the outward one had been.

Classic 'plane-rebalancing' took place, as apparently they had positioned the bags in the hold badly and so we were tipping over, and as a result they had to move some of the passengers around during take-off. They had also got worse with the time issue.

"We will be landing in Melbourne at five minutes past twelve, half an hour behind Alice Springs time."

We arrived at twenty past seven, half an hour ahead of Alice Springs time. We *did* land in *Melbourne* though, so at least they got something right. It was then back to the city for one last night. Australia - done!

Well *actually* not quite...

On the bus back from the airport I was having a discussion with Emma (one of the girls from the flight who had also been on the tour) and I was suggesting some things that she should see in the city. My exciting knowledge and history of tall things obviously impressed her, and before I knew it I had got an invite to a Great Ocean Road-trip. Brilliant! I'd really wanted to do this, but didn't fancy the $100 day tour with the elderly.

She suggested we hired a car tomorrow morning and did it ourselves. So after an unsuccessful night's sleep in my grubby hostel where the toilet flush scared me with its ferocity, I got up at six and joined Emma in the brand new hired Toyota Yaris automatic, and we set off for one last Aussie adventure.

We were soon out of the urban mass of Melbourne and tearing along the Great Ocean Road, driving on some of the most spectacular and fun roads I had ever driven on, with the waves crashing on the sun-drenched rocks below. It was awesome. It was also nice not having to stop every ten minutes for a toilet break as you presumably have to on the guided tour, and as a result we made it to the 'Twelve Apostles' rock formation. The ferocious waves created a dramatic scene as they broke around the bases of the giant sea stacks.

We didn't spend too long on the cliff tops as it was very windy, and we had to get back this evening. It was a thoroughly fun, successful and efficient ten-hour, five hundred kilometre round trip though.

When we got back to Melbourne and had dropped the car off, I headed for the city centre, as I was now homeless.

As it was my last few hours in Australia, I decided to 'live it up' and splash out seven pounds on a glamorous paper-plate-served dinner, and a drink, that for a change wasn't water!

Two Australian women started chatting to me while I was eating, saying how brave I was travelling alone and that my parents must be out of their minds with worry. I decided that this probably wasn't the time to mention my travel history.

Having finished talking to the women, and more importantly my dinner (eating it, not talking to it) I sensed an opportunity. I had found my way into a casino complex. Not since I was sixteen and had gambled twenty-five cents in a Las Vegas casino and then been removed by a large lady with a gun had I had the chance to recklessly throw money away in such a wild fashion.

But I was legal now, and so strode in wearing my scruffy backpacker gear, negotiated my way around the seasoned gambling addicts and sat down in front of the five-cent machines. Well, you have start somewhere...

I didn't win. Well at least I don't *think* I did. I didn't hear the uncontrolled spilling of coins onto my lap as I presume is the indication of success. That was a dollar wasted then. I decided that I wasn't ready for these high rolling machines and so I moved on and hit the two-cent machines.

One of these machines already had an alluring one dollar coin in the prize collection tray, and so I could gamble with someone else's left overs. Ideal.

The machine made excitable winning noises on a few occasions, but it wasn't clear if I had won, and even after repeated tappings on the 'pay-out' button, I left empty handed.

Despite these set-backs, I decided that I was now ready for the big boys, and so went over to the $25,000 minimum bet poker tables. Okay, okay, I went to the $2.50 roulette table, where I slammed down two, five-dollar bills (quietly).

Now in possession of some colourful gambling chips, I placed a five-dollar bet on red. Round and round the ball bearing went, the excitement growing uncontrollably inside me...and then, red! I had won! Success! The sense of glory was amazing.

Now this was a key life moment. Here I could have jumped onto the road to addiction like a cold, starving hitchhiker into a lorry (bear with me, I'm reading a book about hitchhiking) but thanks to my immense will power (and the fact that I needed to catch a bus soon) I stood up, and proudly strode over to the payout till to collect my winnings. I was four dollars up, and I wanted to celebrate.

After a little exploring around the massive casino complex, I found an establishment that catered for just such high rollers, and was soon in the possession (and demolishing) a four-dollar slice of victory cake!

I'm now at the Melbourne's airport, and three hours into a seven-hour wait for my flight via Sydney to Christchurch, New Zealand, and my feet smell mildly of cat biscuits. What a day...

Chapter 9

Hire Cars to Breakfast Bars
Thoughts of an Ice-Trekking Swedish Sea Monster

Day 51

I have arrived in New Zealand! Apparently named after somewhere in Sweden. Presumably called Zealand!

The airport was a nicer experience than entering Australia. I heard they fine you if you have mud on your shoes, but as I only had a light covering of red outback dust on them, they just cleaned them for me. Sadly they said they wouldn't do the same for the rest of my clothes.

I nearly didn't make it any further than the airport though, as the cash machine didn't want to give me any money. Here I was on the other side of the world and I had no legal currency. I could see problems arising. Luckily I found another cash machine in a different terminal building that was more tolerant of my foreign bank card, and I was soon on my way.

Actually that's a lie. It took another half hour to find the bus stop as they had moved it away from the signs. Clever.

So I'm in Christchurch, at a nice hostel with a piano and a self-service herb garden. I hope this is a sign of things to come. I finally got some sleep last night after thirty-six hours of being awake, and I got up late this morning and invested in some warm clothes as it's *freezing* here. It has also been cloudy and dull so far, which I have not been accustomed to lately, and therefore I am currently unimpressed.

Having stocked up on some more layers I made further inroads into my bank account by booking various activities and accommodation for the next couple of weeks. To celebrate the day's successes, I returned to my hostel this evening and packed my stomach full of pasta. It feels good to be full again.

I had another good night's sleep last night, despite a dangerously narrow bunk. (And a girl who kept 'sleep-talk' asking me "How on earth are you going to get the money?" - for which I just kept coming up with ridiculous answers that she didn't appreciate...presumably because she was asleep.) I got up mid-morning and took a bus to Lyttelton, the harbour suburb of Christchurch where you can take a gondola up the mountain. It was now bright blue skies and the views were amazing. New Zealand has hit with a bang.

I eventually found my way out of the gondola station (a surprisingly tricky operation) and then wandered off around the mountains, with spectacular views out across the city, mountains, and the Pacific Ocean. There was no one else around except sheep and cows. Forty million cows apparently, although to be honest I didn't get a chance to count them. I went off the main tracks and had some fun with the self-timer on my camera (even if my selected locations of dangling over cliff edges was a little risky) and then found my way to the remains of a mountain top fort and watched the ships sail in and out of the harbour.

I continued on around the mountain for another half hour or so, before realising it was getting dark, and so I started to head in the direction I thought would take me back to the Gondola station. An hour later and I was safely down the mountain and on the number 16 bus back to the city centre. New Zealand has certainly made a good first impression.

Day 53

After three nights in Christchurch I've now moved four hours up the east coast to Kaikoura. This meant my first Kiwi Experience bus ride. They are like overbearing parents. They book everything for you if you give them half a chance and then deliver you everywhere. This is fine for the type of people who can't tie their own shoelaces, or who panic when they hear that they have 'lost' eleven hours when flying here from the UK (yes, I've heard these stories) but I enjoy the freedom of sorting things out for myself. They *even* hold on to your ticket so you don't lose it. I feel like a rebellious child when I go off on my own, but in case they get worried I have to phone them all the time to tell where I am so they can collect me later. *Sigh*.

Despite the restrictive nature of the bus operation (and their need to stop every ten minutes for a toilet break) it was a brilliant winding coastal road to Kaikoura (meaning; "Eat Crayfish") with snow-capped mountains meeting the sea. More impressiveness.

This evening I had the pleasure of peeling the plastic off the freshly drawn tattoo that was now on the back of a German man in my dorm. I think he must like New Zealand too, as he now has a map of it on his back. I may follow him in case I get lost.

Day 54

I've always been pretty good at getting up in the morning, especially when there is the prospect of fun and adventure. Today should have been one of those days.

I was supposed to be going swimming with dolphins, but after a disturbed night thanks to my Israeli dorm buddy dropping things on me in his sleep from the bunk above all night, and then using a torch beam to infiltrate my sleep while finding them, I wasn't feeling particularly psyched. There was a more significant reason too - it was bloody *freezing*. I've only just adapted to wearing underwear and shoes again, and I still wear thongs wherever possible (and sometimes my flip-flops too!) so the fact that I could see my breath subtly masking the snow-capped mountains out of the window was not an inviting prospect.

But being the massive animal lover I am (ssshh!) I got up, found the Israeli guy in a different bed to the one he started in (strange) and then trekked through the ice caverns to the shower (okay, it was two metres from my room).

Here I faced a predicament. There are two showers. One has no hooks in the cubicle, and so all your stuff gets wet on the floor, while the other has hooks (two would you believe!) but a window that is jarred open, and so the water freezes on your body. I chose the hook-freezer. My stuff fell off the hook and got wet. *Sigh*.

Once I was finally wrapped up in all of my clothes and had consumed a couple of breakfast cereal bars (that I can feel a growing addiction towards) I ventured off to the dolphin centre, taking in the amazing views as I walked. On the way I narrowly avoided getting run over by a man in a car, who presumably found the view of me in the middle of the road taking photos less appealing.

I arrived at the dolphin centre to be told that there was very little chance I would see any dolphins. Right. But they would still charge me if I went. Brilliant. I think I'll take the refund please. So I went and skimmed stones into the sea instead, and after this strenuous activity I walked up the main coastal road through Kaikoura to the supermarket, where I bought some heavily discounted 'pizza bread' that I ate when I got back to the hostel. It was tasty.

Day 55

Today I forgot to take my towel to the shower. Today I also saw a man wearing a suit with a baseball cap, skateboarding down the wrong side of the road whilst carrying a violin.

Day 57

I arrived in Nelson yesterday, at a hostel that lured me in with the promise of free evening soup. It's the backpacker's dream.

After walking about this so called "city" with my dorm buddy Mark, we had our vegetables in water, and then cooked a stir-fry using the free noodles we were given when we checked-in. I think that's the backpacker's equivalent of a mint on the pillow. We were also given free laundry powder. It's all give give give here!

Today I went on a trip to the popular tourist destination of Abel Tasman National Park. It was a dull start to the day, but soon the sun came out and it was a bright sunny day.

It was a two-hour bus journey from Nelson to the National Park, and from there we boarded a ferry for a short ride along the coast. There were only three of us that got off the ferry on a deserted beach in a small cove towards the north of the National Park, and once we had been ditched we began the four hour trek back down the coast.

We wound around the coastal paths, through the rainforest and over the hills to secluded bays in between games of '20 questions' and 'categories'. It turns out that I'm not very good at either. Partly because I have problems counting beyond five so I never knew which question I was on, and partly because asking questions such as;

"Does the person usually carry a suitcase?" is apparently a waste of a turn. Whatever.

On our woodland adventure we came across a deserted wooden hut that had a wood chopping axe outside, so we all chopped some wood with the wood-chopping axe. I like wood chopping, and I like saying it, and *that's* why I've made you read it repeatedly. They probably shouldn't leave things like that lying around though, or at least pay us for our services.

On the trek I started to appreciate my clever day bag that keeps your back cool, even if it is at the expense of making all your things in your bag curved, but I never did quite understand why bag space is measured in litres. Mine says '18 litre' on the front. Does that mean I can pour eighteen litres of clothes in it? It's stupid. That means nothing to me. It would be more useful to know how many pairs of socks I can cram in, or whether I can fit an average-sized family cat in the base compartment. I shall write to the 'Rucksack Standards Agency' on my return.

Despite my moaning about bag-capacity measurement *and* my inability to play basic children's travel games, it was a very enjoyable trek, and with the blue skies and sun glistening off the clear waters as they washed over the golden sands (travel brochure moment...) the three of us were left thoroughly satisfied with our investment in this excursion. The only issue that left us a little confused was the signposting throughout the trek.

It seems that New Zealand's Department of Conservation (DOC) can only work in fifteen minute time intervals, and as a result we passed a lot of signs telling us how far it would be to the next cove or point of interest, but then we arrived a lot quicker than expected.

At one point we passed a sign telling us that it was thirty minutes to the beach, then approximately nine paces further on there was another sign saying that the *same* beach was only fifteen minutes walk! You could still see the *last* sign that said it was thirty minutes! Maybe they just have low expectations of how fast (or lost) tourists can be. I suppose it was pretty hot.

The bus driver that delivered us to and from Abel Tasman was very cynical and bitter about urban development, machine-based industry, and pretty much *anything* modern...even buses ironically.

He also spent a huge amount of time talking about apples. He liked apples. In fact he *loved* apples. He even suggested (or rather demanded) that we visit Versailles, but not for the palace, oh no! ...but for the vegetable patch. He also looked incredibly similar to Harrison Ford. In fact I think he would easily get the lead role in 'Indiana Jones and the Raiders of the Lost Orchard'.

The bus also served as a school bus which was a little odd. Those kids must get seriously bored of hearing about apples.

An exciting moment of the trip came when the medically trained Morag (yes, she was Scottish) managed to diagnose my 'purple hand' problem! Apparently it's called 'Reynaud's Disease'. It's not very catchy (literally) but maybe that will stop people pressing on my hands in cold weather. She also came out with the line of the day, possibly *even* the month;

"I'm not being pernickety, I'm just being right."

Day 58

Today was wet. I'm wet, my clothes are wet - everything is wet. This is only the third properly rainy day I've had in eight weeks of travelling though, so I'm not complaining.

Although actually I *am*, and that's because right now - I'm very wet. I couldn't do the activities I had planned as a result, so instead we sat around the hostel and watched films and cooked things - mainly food, but also the occasional Canadian.

I then got bored of being inside and so I went off, and after walking around the grey and dull streets of Nelson, the weather cleared up a bit, and so I ended up doing what I had intended on doing today anyway.

"Excuse me, how far is it to the centre of New Zealand?" I asked a man and his dog, although it was mainly aimed at the man as his dog looked less knowledgeable.

"Ten minutes." He replied. (The man, not the dog.) Twenty seconds later I found a sign that said it was fifteen minutes. Three minutes later I found a sign that said it was ten minutes, and then five minutes later I arrived at the Centre of New Zealand! More classic sign posting.

The top was impressive - there's a symbolic post and everything! It's also very conveniently located right at the top of a very large hill.

I had just enough time to regret not bringing my camera and to glance out over the misty Nelson and the bay beyond, before running back down the hill again as it was getting dark, and this *definitely* felt like the type of place where people would try and steal your shoes from you whilst you were still wearing them.

Day 61

I've just finished up some more free evening soup. It seems to be quite common in New Zealandish hostels, and very soon I expect to be in the top food-critic circles for my knowledge of vegetable soup.

I'm now further down the West Coast, in Franz Josef - glacier country! I'm currently sitting around a wood burning fire (well I will be when one of my fellow backpackers hurries up and gets it lit!) and relaxing after spending three days with the worst bus group I've been stuck with in two months of bus tripping. It was full of self-involved, egotistical ****s with IBS. (Ignorant Brit Syndrome.) There were a few people on this bus that *were* okay, but most of them left because the others were so bad.

On this particular bus we stopped over for one night in the nothingness that is Westport, and then the following day carried on around the coast, stopping off at Punakaiki, and the Pancake Rocks that it is famed for.

The weather even improved for these dramatic coastal formations as we spent an hour trekking through the dense bushes as we worked our way around the towering layers of rocks (they look like pancakes...*kind* of) with the sea crashing violently into the blowholes that helped erode this geological tourist attraction into shape.

Last night was the 'famous' Kiwi Experience party at Lake Mahinapua. This place is essentially just a pub run by a strange old man called Les. He's 82, and does this party six nights a week, and has been for god knows how long. We were told the party theme was bin-bags, and we were given two accordingly (two bin-bags each that is, not two as a group – that would be tricky to accommodate forty-nine people in two and a half metres of plastic) and a role of tape. We had stopped in grey, grey, Greymouth on our way to the pub so that we could buy additional bits. We then arrived at the pub, and set to work fashioning our bin-bags into whatever we could think of.

A couple of hours later we gathered in the pub for a much-needed steak, pasta, vegetable, and venison stew meal, to which some bright spark said, "I thought we were having deer?" We then returned to our dorms to finalise our outfits.

I had raided the DIY discount bin at our stop-off, so had to skilfully attach my hi-viz jacket, yellow rope, blue knitting wool, gardening gloves, er...white tights (courtesy of Lisa) and bin bags, before being told by my Swedish dorm mates that I looked Swedish, and so I became a Swedish Sea Monster. *Obviously.* The finest Swedish Sea Monster in the land I might add. A view that must have been shared by the barmaid, as after an evening of rustling (of bin-bags, not sheep theft) I won second prize in the best dress-up competition. Well they say every cloud has a silver lining...

We then all drank a lot, and after a disturbed night of people forgetting which room they were in, we set off aboard the green monster (the Kiwi bus) but not before I had got up early to run down to the beach and lake for a quick spot of landscape tourism.

Another spectacular winding road led us further into mountain country, and other than a stop at the 'Bushman Centre', with its angry freshwater eels and funny old men, we were non-stop (well, other the other standard seven or eight 'refreshment' stops) to Franz Josef, for some icy adventures! The scenery (like the fire now - thanks to the German girl) is hotting up, and it's about to get colder!

Day 64

I don't normally write in this thing while I'm on the bus for two reasons; firstly the scenery is always very impressive and so I look out of the window, and secondly it's just too bumpy, and I find it hard enough to write straight as it is. Obviously this is typed so it's not so much of an issue, but I could have misread the scribbles as anythonk.

All this is irrelevant though, as the bus has broken down. We're stranded by the side of the road in a field. But it's not all bad, because it has been more clear blue skies *groan* making the reflections of Mt Cook and Mt Tasman in the still morning waters of Lake Matheson picture perfect. So we took lots of pictures, just like the ones that you see of this definitive New Zealand sight on postcards all over the country.

Day 65

Okay, this is going to screw things up. The bus was fixed quicker than expected, and we arrived in the fantastic lakeside setting of Wanaka yesterday evening. But anyway, back to before...

We arrived in the quaint tourist village of Franz Josef, that lies at the bottom of one of New Zealand's top tourist draws – the Franz Josef Glacier. There are numerous ways that you can choose to see this icy spectacle, and back in Christchurch I had opted for the heli-hike. While this was a serious raid on my bank account I saw it as one of the highlights of the country, and so I considered it a worthy investment.

After a night in a nice little hostel (log fires, free soup – you know the drill) I was up early and heading for the check-in point for the heli-hike. Once there, we kitted up with boots, gloves and jackets before making our way over to the heli-pad. I was very excited. I had never been in a helicopter before, and it was really the main reason I had decided to do this expensive glacier-tour option. It didn't disappoint.

It was brilliant 'choppering' up the valley, and turning horizontal as we wound around the mountains, all whilst we frantically snapped away with our cameras.

Having flown up through the valley above the glacier we landed on the ice. The blinding glare from the sun as the light bounced off the ice temporarily shielded us from the dramatic setting that stretched out before us.

Once we had our vision back through the aid of sunglasses, and we had attached our cramp-ons, we were ready to venture off on the glacier. It was fantastic. We spent three hours trekking over ice columns that towered above us, crawling through cracks and crevices, and battling through caves (can you sense the drama??) all with the assistance of our trusty ice-axes. Sadly they didn't prove as effective as I'd hoped, and I as I was strategically crossing a small gorge between two massive walls of ice, I lost my grip (well *actually* the axe did – it's all the axe's fault) and I fell through the ice and got soaked up to my waist on one side.

It was a little chilly, and I then had to complete the rest of the ice-trek with a boot full of icy water.

After we had found our way back to the pickup point, we jumped back into the helicopter (*obviously* we didn't jump - that would be in violation of civil aviation policies of acceptable procedure) and flew back to Franz Josef. We dropped off our kit at the tour centre and then I returned to my hostel to warm up my foot. Luckily I had chosen to wear the company socks.

The day after heli-hike I decided to a walk up to the base of the glacier from Franz, scrambling along the riverbed (the bits that weren't under water) and jumping over streams, rocks and Japanese people as I went. It turns out that my shoes are waterproof, and I'm very grateful for it. I even helped build a river crossing for some elderly people (Cub Scout badge in the post I presume) although having seen me use it relatively unsuccessfully, they may have opted for a different route.

Two strange nights followed. I was in a six-bed dorm on my own. It had been around six weeks since I was last alone in a dorm and I found it strangely unnerving not to have the rhythmic snores of fellow travellers sending me to sleep/a violent-dorm-massacre-rage. I managed though, and last night there were eight of us rammed into the smallest dorm I've encountered while travelling, so normality was restored.

Day 66

Half way!

I'm now in the attractive lakeside town of Wanaka.

I was just helping an American man upload some photos onto Spacebook. He was moving to New Zealand, and wanted to know how to spell the name of the place he was moving to. He also had some other geography-based questions.

"So, like, where is Singapore?"

"It's on the southern tip of the south-east Asian peninsula." [Blank look] "...on the

end of Malaysia." (I dumbed it down.)

"Oh, so like, is Malaysia, like, a city?"

No. No it isn't. He had just wasted all of his allotted stupid-credits in under a minute, so I left him.

We arrived at the soulless hospital ward stylings of the 'Base' hostel early evening, and then we had to endure the fun of checking in the double Kiwi bus load of 106 backpackers at the same time. It was messy.

Having escaped the brawl at the reception desk I decided to do my usual trip to the supermarket to snap up the discount offers before the old women sneak in and beat me to it.

After a few minutes of rummaging in various aisles across the store, I emerged with a slab of half-price lemon cake.

Result! I took it back to the hostel and was about to start eating it when I overheard some people chatting on the next table. From what they were saying I guessed that they might be Kiwi busers too, and so I was going break the ice (or the cake) with them, and offer them a slice, but then I tried some and it was really nice, so I ate it all. Ah well, I can make friends tomorrow.

Day 67

The sun was out yesterday, and so after shutting my finger in the shower cubicle door I hired a Kayak and went out onto Lake Wanaka. I was the only one out on the massive, perfectly calm lake that was lined by the town on one side, and mountains on the other three.

It was fun splashing about as I paddled across the lake, occasionally balancing my oars on the front as I attempted some 'arty' photos. I've no idea how you take an arty photo, and so they were pretty much just nice shots of mountains with the occasional oar in the way.

After returning to shore and removing my life jacket, I took a stroll along the lakeside, and walked to the end of a jetty to sit on a comfortable looking post. I was not expecting the sight that greeted me. I looked into the clear water to see ducks bobbing up and down on the water (nothing unusual there) but then below them was a large group of freshwater eels (*more* unusual). There were loads of them and they were huge! It was probably therefore best that I only found this out *after* I had been out on the lake, as I've heard they bite.

Later that evening I bumped into Mark who I had first met in Nelson, and after watching the sunset we spent the evening laughing and joking at his less utilitarian hostel. I realise I should have re-phrased that to make it sound more manly and less like a date. We actually played pool and table tennis.

This morning the bus set off for Queenstown, 'the adventure capital of the southern hemisphere' but not before stopping off at 'Puzzling World'. It was a building full of...puzzles. It also had a maze and numerous illusion rooms, which therefore may not have really been there at all! But they were, and they kept us briefly entertained.

It was a pretty good stop overall (better than another roadside cafe stop at least) although I don't want to disillusion you – it was a little...puzzling?? Probably not quite a-maze-ing though. I'll stop.

The next point at which the bus pulled up at was at a bridge over a deep narrow gorge. Here I sensed the perfect opportunity to escape the Kiwi bus, and so I jumped off the bridge. Unfortunately I bounced back up, and wound up back on the bus. Maybe it was for the best though. I'll explain.

I had asked at the bridge-bungee reception if they had the voucher for the bungee photo/dvd package I had won for my dress-up at the party a few days back. They said they had, and so I couldn't *not* do it really. I hate wasting freebies. So they weighed me, and then I wandered out onto the bridge. This was my first view of the drop, and it was quite big.

Within seconds I was being fastened into a harness. I don't know if this was done to scare me, but as he was fastening it, one of the clips broke.

"Ooops, that's not suppose to happen!" He joked. It wasn't very funny.

Anyway, once I was unconvincingly strapped up and had the bungee cord attached to a towel around my legs (yes, nothing unprofessional here) I waddled to the edge of the platform, smiled at the camera, and after a 3, 2, 1 - I jumped.

It's quite the adrenalin buzz as you fall helplessly towards the river, the ground rush giving you that hollow sensation in your stomach, before springing back up, and falling again…and so on.

I hadn't actually considered how you get back once you had finished bouncing, but suddenly I heard a voice shouting "grab the pole!"

What pole? I thought. I'm dangling in mid air, there are no pol...oh. And then a pole came into my vision, being held at the other end by a man in a dingy. So *that's* how it's done!

It was a strange experience, especially when you consider it costs around $70 a second, but probably worth it. Most importantly of all though - I got a free t-shirt, so that will save on washing. You always have to think about efficiency whilst travelling.

A short while later we were back on the bus and arriving in Queenstown. It had started to rain, and it's not supposed to stop anytime soon.

Day 68

It hasn't rained today, but it did snow a bit when I took the gondola up the mountains that surround Queenstown, and as I raced down the hillside luge course in my plastic free-wheeling go-cart, my hands got very cold. Yes mother, I *know* I should have brought my gloves.

After that fast-paced start to the day I returned to the lower heights of Queenstown and went to the lakeside park to participate in a less strenuous activity – Frisbee Golf. This is a novel game that is special to Queenstown. Well, it's a special place...

As with golf, there are eighteen 'holes' (posts or metal chain baskets) and you have to hit the pole/get the frisbee in the basket from the 'tee' with the least Frisbee throws. It was something new which was exciting, but it also got quite repetitive and frustrating, and with the constant risk of accidently frisbeeing a dog-walker's head off, or losing the frisbee in the neighbouring lake, I decided to call it quits.

I then bumped into some of my old bus buddies who were also playing, and we all decided that we had played our part in supporting this niche 'sport', and wandered off into town.

I spent last night hanging around the hostel (no, not in a yobbish/ASBO way — as a resident) where I watched television in the lounge whilst having to endure the loud conversations of other guests. There was one especially loud, fat, middle-aged man with an irritating voice, who clearly loved himself, and enjoyed trying to make sure everyone else in the room knew it. (Cab driver? I thought.) Sadly his co-conversationalists were equally as self-involved.

"So you wanna go out for a quiet night?'

"Yeah, what like last time!"

"Okay...so just four beers?"

"For a quiet night! Try timsing that by four!" (*Surely* a cab driver.)

"So six beers?" (No, I don't get the maths either.)

"Nah, six is an odd number, it will 'ave to be four or eight." (Yup, all logic and rational reasoning has gone out of the window. I'm now also practically chanting 'cab driver' under my breath.)

[Conversation moves on]

"Yeah, I always buy new stuff. I get bored of my stuff and see new ones so I get

them. I want a black and red one." [Snowboard]

"Is that why you have black and red shorts?"

"Yeah, they're black and red - because I like the colour red. And I like the colour black." (You can't argue with his reasoning there...)

"So you make a lot of money then?"

"Nah, not 'ere, but at home." (Nods in a knowing, arrogant fashion.)

"Oh, what is it you do?" (Cab driver, cab driver, cab driver...)

"I'm a cab driver."

BINGO!

I left to go to bed. I was being as quiet as possible, undressing and sorting my stuff in virtual silence so I didn't disturb the others in the room. I finally got into bed; just in time for a gust of wind to blow the curtains open slightly, allowing just enough light from outside into the room for me to see that there was no one else in the room. Dammit!

Half an hour later, everyone else returned noisily to the room, flicking lights on and off and seemingly knocking over anything they could. *Sigh*.

Day 69

Last night I went out for a few beers with some people from my hostel, but not before most of the hostel's residents seemed to gather around the television to watch 'Mean Girls'. Classic. But *I* of course was above all that, and *I* read my book. Well I had my book on my lap. And for some of the time it was open...at a page I probably wasn't on. Well whatever. When we *did* finally go out we ended up in a lively bar that had a live band playing. It was rockin'.

I was up early today to do a touristy tour of Milford Sound, which apparently isn't a Sound, but a Fiord, and is in New Zealand's largest National Park - Fiordland National Park, which could fit all the other National Parks in it, *and* Israel...It all makes sense really.

It was a long bus journey, partly because of the usual collection of toilet stops – including an especially long one at the lakeside town of Te Anue, but mainly because we had to drive three sides of a square to get around all those stupid mountains and lakes. *So* inconvenient. Nice views though.

We drove to around one thousand metres above sea level, and emerged from the clouds to be surrounded by snow, *and* it was snowing! It was quite strange. We stopped off for a brief foray into the snow, and witnessed an Indian tour group apparently experiencing the first snow they had ever seen. I felt privileged that I was part of this with them, even if they *did* get in the way of my photos.

Once back on the road we entered a steep downhill tunnel, before reappearing in daylight without any trace of the snow we had been surrounded by before the tunnel.

A short while later we pulled up at 'The Chasm' (a collection of strangely shaped holes with water flowing through them) and then we arrived at Milford Sound, where we boarded a cruise boat and sailed up and down the fiord, admiring its spectacular vertical cliff faces and waterfalls. We also had a nice buffet lunch.

On the way return leg of the boat trip we briefly stopped to visit an underwater observatory, where we...observed under the water. Apparently the observatory consisted of nineteen windows! No, I *didn't* count them, but yes, that *was* about as exciting as it got. We then got back on the bus and drove back to Queenstown. I realise I've just made that fourteen hour trip sound quite short, but we did spend about twelve hours of it on the bus.

Chapter 10

Hot Tubs and Seal Cubs
Thoughts of a Wind-Swept Sky Captain

Day 72

I'm now back in Christchurch and I'm furious. If only you could see me now. My cheeks are puffed out and red (and not just because of the cold) and I would be frowning heavily. I'm so angry that I can't think of an angrier expression than a heavy frown.

I'm not furious because I'm back in Christchurch though, it's a nice place, but because I arrived at the soup pot in the kitchen to find it empty. It was four minutes past six. Four minutes past six!! That's four minutes past the hour of official soup readiness! I was outraged.

No longer do I choose my hostels based upon their proximity to disease ridden prostitutes and drug vendors (mind you, I did pass a lovely young lady who was dressed rather inappropriately for the season on the street corner last night whilst on my way back from the evenings bargain-raid at the local 'Pak 'n' Save') but I have made the difficult switch to basing my residences on whether they offer free evening soup. So to be denied this now established basic human right of a backpacker hurts. It hurts deep. So I cried. Actually I think that was more down to the fact that someone was chopping onions next to me. Anyway, I got over it how I knew best, by binge-eating 250 grams of pasta and half a broccoli. Seriously though, I now have to question what I'm doing at this hostel.

Okay, maybe that's a little melodramatic, but last night I got seconds! *And* it was the best free soup I'd had on this trip so far! It was so good I actually choked on it whilst trying to talk to someone. Luckily she mothered me well, and she brought me a glass of water. Not my finest introduction admittedly. Maybe I'm going on about soup a bit too much, but now I've completed the south island loop I have less to write about.

This hostel does have some interesting features though. Next to my top bunk is a power socket that is only for shavers. I've never shaved in bed before, but this feature seems to actively encourage it. Hmmm, I'll keep you posted. It also has a cat! I think that this is a brilliant addition to a hostel. After Australia's ridiculous portfolio of animals that can *all* kill you (crocodiles, jellyfish, sharks, receptionists, etc) to see something as mundane as a domestic cat is very welcome. Even if it does currently occupy the last seat in the lounge, so as a result I'm out in the corridor.

* * *

For my last night in Queenstown I went out with various people from my hostel, and others who I had met from around the south island. It was an enjoyable affair, and I even had a 'legendary' 'Fergburger'.

This is the gourmet burger that has a cult status around these parts, especially among royals and dignitaries (drunken backpackers). It's actually really nice, and *not* covered in grease as you may expect, but instead filled with huge amounts of...whatever they fill it with.

So I have now joined the masses in its endorsement, and to be honest I feel a little disappointed about that, as I like to be different. Because they say it *pays* to be different. No one's *ever* paid me though, and in fact these people are probably the same people who also say 'if a job's worth doing, it's worth doing properly'. However I've always found that 'a rushed job is a done job'. But I guess that's neither here nor there.

I did have some onion rings though, whereas most people have chips. So I *am* different. Phew.

The next morning was an eight-hour bus that took me back here to Christchurch, passing through the snow-covered Southern Alps and more lakes. Obviously we didn't pass *through* the lakes - that would be stupid and we'd all get wet feet - but we went *near* them, and took photos of them.

Tomorrow I think I'm going to buy a new pen. The adventure continues!

Day 74

I haven't bought a new pen.

Yesterday was a bright sunny day, and so I took the bus to Lyttelton as I had done on my last visit, but this time I went paragliding!

This was hugely exciting, as not only did it involve gliding a kilometre above Christchurch with the backdrop of snow-covered mountains and the Pacific Ocean, but it also meant that I now not only knew the *difference* between hang gliding, paragliding, and parasailing, but I had now *done* them all! So it was mission complete.

I'm aware I hadn't mentioned this *was* a mission of mine, but trust me, it was, and it is now therefore complete. So there.

The paragliding instructor met me at the bus stop next to the gondola base station, and then we drove into the Lyttelton mountains where I had been exactly three weeks ago today. That day. Yesterday...oh, you get the idea. We then climbed over a fence into a field of sheep, and essentially ran off the mountain whilst I was strapped to a backpack that I *sort of* sat in once airborne.

We spent over half an hour swirling around in the air thermals above the mountains while I tried to take photos with gloves on. It's quite tricky. The views were stunning though. The sky was even clearer and brighter than it had been last time, and obviously it helped that I was up in the sky. And we all know that everything looks better when you're up in the sky.

As we descended into the field for our return to earth, I made a strategic attempt to land on a sheep and sheep-surf back down the mountain. Sadly this didn't happen, and I'd hate to mislead you. No, in fact we bumped down relatively smoothly into the field we had taken off from, and then he drove me down to the bottom of the mountain and dropped me somewhere where I had no idea where I was.

Luckily I'm lightning sharp (no, I'm not convinced that is a phrase either) and so I quickly worked out which way I should be heading. I found a bus stop nearby, but then got bored of waiting, and so ended up walking back.

It took two hours, which included a small detour via 'Pak 'n' Save' where it said it was 'Wacky Wednesday'. Now that sounded exciting! I had mental images of clowns riding around the aisles on unicycles whilst simultaneously juggling heavily discounted cakes...but it wasn't to be. In fact there was nothing 'wacky' about it at all! The only thing of note was a very bored looking security guard who was kicking an empty box. Rubbish. Literally. So I left.

* * *

Now I know what you're thinking; all this throwing myself off bridges and running off mountains is all a *bit* high risk and active, and that I should probably take some time out from this stressful lifestyle to relax. Well you'll be pleased to know that last night I did just that.

After freeing myself from the paws of the resident cat (who seemed to take a shine to my fleece and started pawing at it, inadvertently giving me a strange sort of stomach massage) I got into the hostel's hot tub. It was very hot. And I suppose quite tubbish while we're on the subject.

I was then joined by the Scottish lads who I keep meeting around the south island, so there were soon five of us in there. I'm pretty sure it was a four-man tub. There were legs *everywhere*. Well at least I think they were legs. They may have been freshwater eels. Whatever was in there, it was still pretty relaxing, if a little cold when we got out. But then everything has its drawbacks.

I overheard a fat American lady on the bus to Lyttelton the other day. Actually there are two things wrong with that. Firstly, I didn't 'overhear' her being fat. I strained my neck to observe her, as a result of the second inconsistency with the original statement, being that I didn't 'overhear' her, but I couldn't 'under hear' her, as she was talking so bloody loudly.

Anyway, the point is that she said something very interesting. Again, I'm playing it pretty loose with the term 'interesting', but I'm guessing you want me to shut up and get to the point by now.

Apparently the most popular boys name in the United States is Jason, and has been for the past ten years. I thought that this was an important fact that I should share with you. I'm sure it's the truth too, because fat people are reliable sources. Reliable sources who eat reliable sauces. I know that makes no sense. I was trying to be clever with words but it didn't materialise.

Okay, I lied. That wasn't very interesting, but it still may be the type of fact that saves you at an important dinner party – and whom will you have to thank? That's right - me. Or fat, bus-seat-disfiguring Americans. Oh, and before the anticipation overwhelms you, the most popular girls name is Emily. Apparently. I'll be testing you on that when I get back.

Day 77

It's Sunday, so you should be resting, or gardening, or ironing your shirt for work tomorrow. Of course if you're Norwegian you might be recovering from a massive, record-breaking Eurovision win induced hangover. And congratulations to you for that. (The win, not the hangover.)

I'm now back in Kaikoura and at a hostel that a few people had recommended to me. It's not hard to see why, as it's probably the nicest hostel I've stayed in. Its special features include 'Turkish' style bunks that have bamboo sidewalls and a dignity curtain! I selected one of these novel beds, forgetting that most beds are six foot long (and three foot four wide...don't ask why I know that, because I don't know) and as I'm six foot one (and a little bit) I have an inch (and a little bit) that won't fit in.

BUT after some careful algebra (Pythagoras' Theorem: a2 + b2 = c2) I established I could fit in diagonally along the hypotenuse (I know I'm cool.) That basic maths also served to help send me to sleep. Along with *Lord of the Rings* films of course. Luckily I had spent the first year of university sleeping diagonally thanks to a badly placed, built-in wardrobe, so I adapted pretty quickly.

They also have 'proper' free coffee here, which is brilliant!...except I don't drink coffee, but I still saw it as a positive. One of the other attributes to this hostel that *did* lure me in though (dignity curtains aside) was the herb shelf.

As a traditional backpacker, I eat a sh*t load of pasta, and as I discovered at university, herbs greatly enhance pasta meals. The problem came when I got to the herb adding stage of the pasta production process last night, and I had built up the herb selection and adding part so much that the excitement of the occasion got to me and caused me to panic. I ended up using parsley, which I'm fairly sure *isn't even* a herb! But it was nice all the same.

Tonight I'm living it up and breaking the pasta-trend, and having a (price-reduced) steak! This is very exciting. I think I'm going to marinade it with herbs and spices. I don't even really know what 'marinade' means, but will assume it means 'add stuff until it smells different'. I'm also going to have a pepper. Yup, I'm quite the cooksman.

Last night we were sitting around the wood-burning fire playing cards. (Can you feel the stress levels?)

"So what did you do today?"

"I went swimming with dolphins. How about you?"

"I climbed a mountain and went seal watching. What did you do?"

"I flew a plane."

I get the feeling that these types of conversations won't happen as often when I'm back home. And yes, I was the third person in that conversation. None of that 'swimming' or 'watching' lark - I flew a plane! This was the main reason for my extended return to Kaikoura, as the pilot was on holiday when I was here last time.

The night before last we were sitting around chatting with the couple that own the hostel - Mark and Ruth, and a man called Nick, who turned out to be the 'fly-a-plane' pilot. This was a little concerning in terms of the alarming rate he was knocking back the beers, given that we were flying in less than twelve hours, but come the next day, and when dressed in his flight costume/uniform, he looked far more capable. Not that this was very important as he didn't really do much - he lets you do practically *everything*, including all the controls (flaps/throttle) for take-off and landing. It was amazing.

He had said in the pre-flight briefing (a two minute chat involving a toy plane) that;

"It's just like driving a car really."

I question whether he has a driving licence. I've certainly never driven a car with wings or a propeller. Or one with an axe under the seat for that matter.

"Ah, that's good, you've got your trusty axe with you." I remarked, as I got into the jumbo jet...or similar, and noticed it under the seat.

"Yes. In case you don't let go of the controls when I ask and I have to chop your hands off."

"Excellent."

Luckily it wasn't needed, as I successfully took-off in full control of the throttle and flaps, and flew over the Kaikoura peninsula and the Pacific Ocean. It was a fantastic feeling being at the controls of a plane, and there was the added excitement of getting battered by the strong winds and pulling G-force banked turns and drops. It was brilliant. Actually I invite you all to come over next week and have a go yourselves. He'll appreciate the publicity.

Today was pretty tame in comparison. I just went for a long walk (well it is Sunday) to the seal colony. I had tried to get to walk to this last time I was here, but found I hadn't quite gone far enough. A bit of advice there - always check the map *before* you go, and not when you get back.

It took me around an hour before I was greeted by the uninspiring sight of the seal colony. Seals are boring and smell funny. A bit like my socks actually, except my socks are more functional.

I then carried on over to South Bay on the other side of the headland. It was very windy, and I nearly fell off.

This hostel also has a guitar that has kept me thoroughly entertained in the times when I haven't been out moaning about seals or getting swept of hilltops. I spent two hours yesterday evening messing about on it (playing it, not drawing on it or jumping on it). Seriously, it's stressful times out here.

Actually the seven-tier recycling bin system does cause me a headache. You also have to light the hob with a match (which I've found to be tricky, especially with my strangely flammable fingers) and I can't find a 'wood' bin. Luckily I'm adaptable, and have created a 'wood' pile. It's caught on too, now everyone piles *their* used matches there as well! I think it's probably because I'm hyper-cool and fashionable. I'm sure you'll agree. Right, enough of that, this steak isn't going to marinade itself!

Day 79

We're currently powering across the Cook Strait from Picton to Wellington in a ferry that has clearly been pinched from the English Channel, with 'Portsmouth' and 'Cherbourg' having been tippexed out on the side of the vessel, and replaced with 'Interislander' instead. Clever name.

This is indeed the ferry that transports you from the South Island to the North Island (or the other way round, you know…if you're that way inclined). It's a three-hour trip that takes you through to New Zealand's capital, also known as "The Windy City" as the girl next to me just told me. The nickname that is, not that the ferry goes to Wellington. That would have been careless of me not to have known that before boarding.

My last evening in Kaikoura was really good. Mark and Ruth cooked us all a group meal, and we all sat around the large dining table and ate a vegetarian curry. It was accompanied by some expensive 'limited edition' wine that one of the other guests had brought back from his work on a nearby winery, having recently switched careers from accounting to...wine...business.

We then moved around the fire, where we ate high-quality chocolate and sipped 'pudding wine' whilst playing 'Jenga'. What was nice (was the chocolate masking the unpleasant taste of the overly sweet "pudding" wine) was the atmosphere that had been created by the small group of seven of us (guests and owners) who were all there for the same few days.

Soon the guitars came out, and we strummed away in between discussions about travelling, world politics, and Cray fish fishing. Mark also came out with the fact of the day - maybe *even* the fact of the year.

Apparently more people are alive in the world today than have ever died in the history of the world. There. Try absorbing *that* after a few sips of pudding wine.

Chapter 11

Bad Habits and Shaved Rabbits
Thoughts of a Jay-Walking Master Chef

Day 80

Well I haven't done a 'Michael Palin' and made it around the world in 80 days, but I have made it halfway round, and he had a camel - I only have the Kiwi bus, and the bus stops more often.

I've spent the day walking around New Zealand's capital, and I can see why they call it "the Windy City" - I had to wear a hat! I walked along the harbour front to the parliament building and the "Beehive", and went inside to find that the government was on holiday. How inconvenient. A member of staff asked if I wanted to go on the tour, but as I was happy wandering about myself, I politely declined. I think I must have said it with a slightly suspicious tone that suggested I secretly wanted to overthrow the government with my strategically hidden barrel of gunpowder, as the man gave me a dodgy look, quickly followed by a visitor's sticker. He then left me to it.

After I had finished, I left (which served to emphasise the completion of the visit, and thus satisfying the 'finishing' criteria of the event) and I walked through the city's streets that were full of people in silly hats. These were either innovative head attachments that disperse the strong wind gusts - or it was a university graduation day.

While I was walking back from my governmental experience I was making my way along a busy street when I noticed an empty bus pulled up by the pavement. On the board that usually states the intended route or destination, it simply read "Sorry". It didn't say "Sorry, not in service" as you might expect, just "Sorry". I liked it. The "Sorry" bus.

It seemed to be carefully positioned in the bustling heart of the city to apologise for its diminished functionality in its role as public transport. Or maybe it was a pre-emptive apology for any inconvenience that may be encountered whilst utilising such a service, whether that was being stuck in endless traffic, delayed in arrival and therefore disrupting onward journeys and activities, or the seeming requirement for you to be stuck next to an elderly woman while she openly discusses her various ailments as her overbearing thighs make rapid inroads onto your side of the seat. *Maybe* it was because it had been parked in such a bloody inconvenient place in the road. Well, whatever the reason - I'm sorry too.

I then saw a sign for Wellington's famous cable car that I had been heading for. At least I *assume* it's famous —

although the sign was pretty much my first clue to its existence.

I followed it up a narrow alleyway and found myself in a jewellery shop. This didn't look right. I don't like jewellery shops either. They're so sparkly it makes everything seem hazy, and so I got out as quickly as my dazed vision would allow. I then found myself back on the street again, and right back next to the sign. Was it a trick sign? I tried again, and walked back up the alleyway, *once again* passing the newspaper vendor, who I *once again* had to decline a newspaper from, and therefore demonstrating why he was only a street salesman, as it had only been thirty seconds since my last passing.

Mind you, I was the one who had gone past him in a loop twice in thirty seconds, taking two attempts to notice the cable-car kiosk that was situated in the middle of the alleyway. So swings and roundabouts really. In my defence it *was* very dark.

The cable-car ride itself was a little disappointing. It strained up the hill through various grubby back streets and industrial areas at a painfully slow speed. The views from the top out across the city and bay were pretty good though, as were the Botanic Gardens that I passed through on the walk back down. All cities in this part of the world seem to have 'Botanic' gardens. I should really find out what 'Botanic' means. For now I'm going to assume that it means the parks have lots of misleading pathways.

Once I had finally navigated my way out of the park (the benefit of it being on a hill meant I just kept needing to head downwards) and I had escaped the clutches of Wellington's home of bizarre and frankly disturbing 'sculptures', I went to 'Te Papa', which is Wellington's equivalent of the Science Museum in London.

It's very big, and very interactive. I got to press buttons, switch switches and everything! It sometimes got a little too technical though, and I had to concede defeat to the young Wellingtonians. I'm sure that's what they're called. I also saw the massive squid that someone on one of my earlier bus journeys had gone on about. It *was* pretty big too.

I think it's important to point out that it was a model (*of course* I wasn't actually expecting to see a live one...). In fact I don't think anyone has ever seen a live one – they're just too crafty, and know how to avoid getting stuck in canals or caught up in fishing nets. It would take a bloody big net anyway, this thing was huge! It was also slightly unrealistically displayed, hanging from the roof. I'm sure it can't fly, or survive without water. Yes, it has to be wet. It can't be a *damp* squid.

And yes, that *is* what I thought the phrase was. Because if something is described as a 'damp squid' it's a disappointment, as a damp squid isn't happy (because it wants to be *fully* wet and in the sea) and will therefore not fulfil your expectations of a squid.

I've since investigated, and apparently a 'squib' is a small packet of explosives that wouldn't ignite if it was damp. So a damp quid would actually be a damp squib. Just like this paragraph really…

I hope you've learnt something. I certainly have. I also think I've gone off topic.

I then made my way back to my hostel, having to pass through yet another series of traffic light-controlled junctions. I hate the grid systems here. And in Australia. *And* in America. London is a huge and busy city, and *that* manages with more reasonable crossing networks, so why can't other cities?

I hate the way you have to wait at these crossings while they beep irritatingly and incomprehensibly at you. A lady I met in Singapore had told me that in Australia it was a $100 spot fine if you're caught crossing on a red signal, or if you jaywalked. I had always imagined jaywalking to be a kind of 'cocky swagger' done to a funky bass line and backbeat. In reality it isn't as exciting though, and definitely not worth doing at $100 a pop. I might demonstrate my 'J-walk' (as I've just decided to call it) when I'm back. I firmly believe that it will start a new form of road-crossing movement.

Day 82

I'm in Taupo, which sits on the edge of Lake Taupo, which is New Zealand's largest lake. Apparently it can fit Singapore in it, but presumably not its hyper-efficient MRT subway system as the lake is quite shallow. It is in fact a volcanic crater lake that sits above sea level, and is fed through hot springs, as this is a geothermal region. I even put my hand in a stream and burnt my fingers as it was so hot! Crazy times.

New Zealand's South Island is formed from the pushing together of the Australasian and Pacific plates, whereas the North Island is a volcanic island. This piece of geological insight comes as a result of a reasonably uneventful day.

Yesterday's drive from Wellington was a pretty spectacular trip through the Tongariro National Park, with its distinctive snow covered volcanoes (that were used in a certain set of films that I'm not going to mention).

When we arrived in Taupo I found out that the weather had been rubbish for the past two weeks, but today it was clear blue skies, and so I decided *it was time*.

Well actually I had decided that tomorrow would be time, but time had to be moved forward due to the unpredictable weather.

So less than two hours later I was flying at 12,000 feet and wearing two jumpers and a Kiwi man. Now it was *literally* time. They opened the door to the -25 degree sky, and I jumped out of the plane. Well okay, I fell out. This was the pinnacle of my sky bound adventures, and it was *brilliant*. I was skydiving!

It was surprisingly calm as we fell at 200 kilometres per hour towards the ground, and I was in total awe of the amazing sunset over Lake Taupo. The only interruption to those fantastic forty-five seconds of free-fall came when the photographer kept flying in front of me to take photos and to shake my hand. I even stuck my tongue out at him. He just took a photo of it. And no, it's not a pretty photo.

There was then a sudden yank as the parachute was released, followed by a six-minute float back to earth (with a few G-force turns thrown in for good measure) before landing crotch first into a gravel trap. A rough ending to a fantastic experience. Even if my nose was a little frosty at the end.

While I was waiting to go in the hanger (skydiving – not to the toilet) a man approached me.

"Adam?"

"No." I replied. Unhelpfully, judging by his reaction.

[Next person]

"Is it Adam?"

"No, it's Chris." Well persistence usually pays off...

[Next person]

"You must be Adam."

"Yes, I'm starting to think that too. I can be if it will speed up the paperwork."

"Er...no, we really need Adam."

Yes I got that impression.

[Finally they accept me as Chris and things start to progress]

"Oh, you don't have a harness on." Said as if it was my fault...

"No, but it's okay, I don't think I need one."

The woman laughs, the man is less keen for me to get away with it.

"So what are you gonna do then?!"

"Just whip out this carrier bag that I presume is in this pouch you've attached to me, and float gracefully back to earth."

"No, that's your life jacket."

"Oh."

Right, I'm just wondering at what point during a skydive does slipping on a life jacket become possible. Also, why should you need it? After over 6,000 jumps can they really mess up the route that badly? And attaching it whilst you're strapped to someone else and falling at 200 kilometres an hour must be a little tricky.

* * *

Having been dropped off back at my hostel after this exhilarating activity, I spent the evening in the lounge chatting to an absolutely hammered Maori couple, a massive Maori man (who kept telling me that when I went to Brazil I would wake up in a bath tub full of ice with my kidneys missing) and Doug.

Doug was an American graduate teacher who spent the evening working his way through a tub of peanut butter using his finger. Doug was camped in the garden, and so as I was the only other proper guest, I had a dorm to myself.

The dorm was freezing, partly down to it not having any other people in it to warm it up, and partly down to the fact that it was *very* cold outside. It did have a strip-heater on the wall, but this only managed to warm up the four inches that surrounded the metal grill. Luckily my trusty sleeping bag liner came to the rescue once again.

The only real event of today came when I went to the local Pak 'n' Save and found (having paid for my shopping) that you had to *buy* carrier bags. Not only that but you had to pick them up at the *start* of your shop! Was this some kind of a sick joke?! I was now past the checkouts! I was stranded!

I eventually managed to pinch an empty cardboard box from a skip in the entrance hall, and then I had to pack my food into that and carry it for the forty-minute walk back to the hostel. No one wants to be seen walking through town with a cardboard box under their arm, but what wouldn't have helped my homeless image was eating dry bread out of my box as I walked along the lake because I was so hungry. Ah, there's no shame when you're backpacking.

Day 83

Today - nothing has happened. Actually I got stalked around the hostel by a cat this morning. I also burnt some pasta to the bottom of the pan this evening while I was waiting for the kettle to boil. They say a watched kettle never boils -

well this one really never did! I then had to spend the rest of the pasta cooking process fishing out the burnt bits.

So again, today - nothing happened.

Day 84

I was up at 5.30 this morning for the long walk along the lake with all my stuff to get the next bus. It turned out to be a car, and I was the only one in it. I was personally chauffeured! Actually I was taken to a petrol station in the middle of nowhere, and then dumped, before someone else turned up to take me the rest of the way.

In this second chauffeured stretched limousine (rusty van) there was another traveller already inside. His name was also Chris. The chirpy young lady who was driving us decided that having two passengers called 'Chris' was far too confusing, and it would therefore be easier to label us to make us more distinguishable. So he became 'Chris A' (as he was first in the van) and I was 'Chris B'. I didn't have the heart to break it to her that this new method of distinction was actually far more confusing to me. Bless her, she just looked so proud at her clever system.

* * *

172

I'm now sitting on a bed. A *proper* bed! No bunk above me or below me. Somehow I've wound up in a twin room. There's even a picture on the wall! I'm out of my depth.

This is Waitomo - meaning 'Waterhole'. It is a village with a population of forty-one, and I suspect most of those regret being there. The main hotel is now derelict and the village shop closed long ago. It doesn't help that it has been raining either. Things never look that great in the rain.

The reason I'm here (or why anyone comes here) is for the glow worm caves that are believed to be over two million years old. That's roughly the same amount of time it felt like I stayed in Waitomo.

Now there are some exciting ways of seeing them; for instance; you can abseil down a gap in the rocks and fox-fly through them (I have no idea what that is, but my god it sounds exciting!) or you can go black water rafting, which also sounds fantastically dangerous and fun.

But no, none of this I could do. For financial reasons I had to do the 'spellbound' trip, which was as boring and as 'little-girl-waving-fairy-wand-to-the-sound-of-a-triangle' dull as it sounds.

Besides me, there was only a young Australian family to accompany the ageing, tight short-wearing tour guide on this trip. We were taken on a bumpy drive over the undulating limestone hills to a cave entrance, where we floated through the cave in a dingy that had a few worms in (the cave, not the dingy) and then walked through another one.

There were indeed a lot of glow worms, and they dimly lit the caves like a vast collection of LEDs, but in all honesty it wasn't worth the two-day detour. I'm definitely *supposed* to claim that it was 'magical', but I think the reality is that skydiving is more the style of activity I enjoy. Our guide was also a little strange, and I wasn't entirely comfortable being in a dark cave with him.

6.32pm

I'm now waiting for my washing to dry in the dryer, as I realised earlier that I hadn't done a wash for a while. It's mainly socks that suffer the most, and it's hard to justify a sock-only wash. I *was* hoping that by cleaning myself regularly, *my* cleanness would eventually rub off onto my clothes... It hasn't quite worked.

7.21pm

I'm now waiting for my washing to dry in the dryer. Having gone to collect my washing I found that I hadn't pushed the start button, which as it turns out is an integral part of the drying process. Yes, I am an idiot.

Day 85

I'm in Rotorua - land of plenty! Okay, I made that catchy tag line up, but seeing as it has more than two streetlights under it's list of facilities, it beats Waitomo. Not that Waitomo isn't a happening place; it was just a bit...well, crap.

I did go for a walk in the countryside before leaving this morning, only to be stopped in my tracks by a bull that was standing directly on the path on the steep hillside ahead of me. He was looking at me very angrily. I went a bit sheepish and went back. Only kidding, that's a load of bull (I thought) and *then* I left. Okay, enough horsing about, this is getting udderly ridiculous. Now I've lost my train of thought, and *that's* not even a farmyard animal joke!

There was one redeeming feature to my visit to Waitomo. At 12.45 I went to see the only other attraction in the village; the shaving of the rabbit.

I have to say that when our driver first mentioned it yesterday, I was a little intrigued. So as I still had a couple of hours until I was rescued, I wandered over to the sheering shed, where I witnessed something...not *magical*, but *certainly* unexpected.

Every day at 12.45 they shave a German Angora Rabbit. Apparently this has to be done every three months; otherwise the rabbits overheat and die. They then use the fur that they have shaved off to make hats and jumpers.

And sure enough at 12.45, out came Janice. There was then a look of utter bemusement on the faces of the small selection of spectators that had gathered in the room, as they strapped her into a rack, and stretched her to smooth out her skin creases. Janice is the rabbit by the way; I don't know what the woman was called.

They then proceeded to shave off all her fur with a sheep-shearing razor (again, I'm talking about the rabbit here) while those around her took photos. It was the most disturbing yet *hilarious* thing I've seen while travelling. They *even* rotated her on the rack using a handle, *and* shaved off her whiskers! Don't worry though - it's RSPCA approved! But rest assured I also took pictures as evidence.

The rest of the day was uneventful, but then it would be after that. I just sat on the bus while everyone else inevitably fell asleep within minutes, leaving me to watch the mountains out of the window while listening to music and thinking about angry, furless rabbits.

I think it's important to point out the driver was awake too; otherwise I'd be writing this from a ditch somewhere along highway one. She would have a nightmare trying to identify the bodies, what with 'Chris B' turning out to be 'Chris A'.

Day 88

And so whilst the sun did shineth, the green monster of the kiwi did ride forth and yonder, and unto the city that hath sails.

After a few uneventful days in Rotorua that consisted of little more than me ambling around the town and trying to work out if that strange smell was the sulphur coming from the thermal springs or that man sitting next to me on the park bench, I got the bus to Auckland. "The City of Sails" (so called because apparently one in five people here own a boat) is comfortably New Zealand's largest city, with over 30% of the country's population living here.

My hostel is in the centre of the CBD, and I can watch the lifts going up and down the Sky Tower - the tallest building in the Southern Hemisphere - from my bunk in the next block over. There is also a notice blue tacked to the window saying 'Please don't throw rubbish out of the window.' It made me wonder what kind of a problem it must have been to warrant such a sign, and if the people who *were* doing it would really be stopped by a sign. I mean *surely* they can't have ever thought that this was actually the correct method of rubbish disposal?!

While I waited for the bus to Auckland this morning I saw a van with 'Post Haste' written on it, and below that was written 'Delivering excellence - people'.

I think delivering excellence is a great entrepreneurial idea, but I don't think you need a van for it. Delivering people *would* require a van, but it seems a little risky to openly advertise it, as I'm pretty sure people smuggling is illegal.

We stopped off for half an hour in a town called 'Matamata', or to some people 'Hobbiton' (some film set apparently) but to me that Doesntmata.

During our brief stop here, a Maori man shouted at me across the street, saying;

"Do the Haka, that'll keep ya hands out ya pockets - but maybe ya tongue'll freeze!"

He had a thick accent and he seemed angry with me, although I couldn't work out why. This was a strange place. I got back on the bus.

Auckland was recently voted the fourth best city to live in, in the world. It has a population of around 1.4 million, all of which seem to want to leave it at 5pm. It gets *very* busy, and they have the daunting grid junction crossings that I'd first found in Brisbane and Christchurch. You can cross in all directions, and so you have people cutting in front of you, and just generally heading at you from all directions. It's a scary event, especially with the added pressure of having to weave your way through all the people *and* make it to the other side before the bleeping stops and an angry bus ploughs you down. I miss Waitomo.

Oh no, wait! I don't. Sorry Waitomo.

Day 89

Nothing of note happened today, except I got lost in a massive and confusing branch of Borders. I managed to navigate my way across Brisbane at night (while under-the-influence) *and* having only been in the city for eight hours, but here it took nearly as long to get from 'teen fiction' in the basement to 'home cooking' on the second floor. *Neither* of these sections was the one I was looking for.

I also got stuck in a lift in another building, visiting seven floors before finding the right level to exit on. It turned out it was only a five-storey building. It was a tiring day.

In the evening I went out for a meal (first time in New Zealand!) and choose a place that lured me in with their neatly stacked selection of Yellow Pages and phone directories in the glass food-cooler display unit at the front. To be honest the cuisine didn't quite live up to quality that this presentation suggested.

Day 90

It was another 5.30 start for my penultimate Kiwi bus trip to Paihia - Bay of Islands. Annoyingly I was woken an hour early by a Japanese woman who mistook my right foot for a bonus rung of the ladder as she descended from the bunk above me. Glad to be of assistance!...I didn't say.

It was a nice bus ride, and we even got to see some 'shirafs' (a cross breed – I'll let you work out of what). We also passed a farm where the farmer had tried to adjust to the increasing economic pressures of world recession by spray-painting his sheep bright pink in an attempt to make them a tourist attraction. Genius.

Paihia is an attractive little town in the northern tip of New Zealand in the Bay of Islands. Unfortunately my bed in the hostel here is tricky to get into, as the top bunk is so low. I have to essentially adopt a horizontal position before sliding myself in. All part of the fun though. As is meeting other people in the dorm, such as the French guy in the bunk above, who when I first entered the room, jumped up from his bed and enquired what time I was planning on going to bed. It was 1.15pm. Not yet I told him.

Day 93

After three nights of listening to the enchanted snores of the Frenchmen, I'm now preparing for my *final* Kiwi Experience bus! I'm going to miss that bright green, six-wheeled box of hung over Brits. Just like I'm going to miss smacking my head on the bunk above me.

It's been a casual few days in the Bay of Islands, by which I mean that I haven't done much besides going on walks by the bay, and not that I've been strutting around in Doc Martins and open-collared shirts.

Each evening I went down to the beach for the sun set, and last night I even wrote 'NZ' (can you guess what it stands for?!) in the sand to add to my photo setting.

I was intrigued then, that after wandering further down the beach having utilised my inventive sand markings, I looked back to see a much more professional looking photographist with a much more fancy camera using my carefully crafted, cryptic sand markings for her own photos!

I'm sure that outburst of alliteration demonstrates my surprise too. I suppose I should have charged her a usage fee, but I was hungry, so instead I went back to the hostel and cooked a stir-fry.

Today's big event was getting a haircut. I was starting to look homeless and scruffy and had noticed the resultant drop in discounts offered to me.

I happened to pass a suitable place (it said 'haircuts' on a board outside) and spoke to the woman on the desk. She looked like a heroin addict. In fact her depressed gaze through bloodshot eyes made her look like a heroin addict who hadn't had any heroin for a while and was in desperate need of some heroin.

I asked if I needed an appointment and she said yes. I asked her what the earliest time was, and she said today at twelve. Right, so in twenty minutes. It probably wasn't *quite* as busy as she would have liked to make out then.

Anyway, I promised to try and find her some illicit substances that she could inject into herself so she could get a fix, and then I returned at twelve to have my haircut by a woman who looked far less as though she was going to cut my nose off and sell it on for drugs.

Day 96

This is my last evening in New Zealand before flying off to the Southern Americas!

The last few days in Auckland have been bright, sunny affairs, and so I've been wandering about the city, going up and down its hilly, volcanic streets and parks.

I went up the Sky Tower (the Southern Hemisphere's tallest building) for panoramic views across the city. I spent over an hour at the top, gazing out across the clear blue skies and cityscape to the surrounding islands, extinct volcanoes and harbours. You can see both sides of the island from up there, but that's not so surprising given that it is the narrowest point of New Zealand.

The day before yesterday I watched a live band playing in one of the city's squares, and yesterday I watched a large cruise liner being loaded up with provisions and the elderly.

The evenings have been filled with various films in the hostel's television room. Some full of action, some adventure, some made you think, some made you laugh, and some…well, some were just plain stupid. I mean, have you seen 'Penelope'?!

I also risked a return to the local branch of Borders, where I undertook a solid twenty minutes of research into

182

how to get from Santiago's airport to the city centre, then on to my hostel, and then to the hotel where my South American trip would begin a couple of days later. This involved flicking through a Chile guidebook, and scribbling down a few road names, as well as an incredibly technical map drawing (a few free-hand lines on the back of a bus ticket) to help me find and get to where I was supposed to be. Job done.

This evening I went down to the kitchen to cook the same meal I had cooked yesterday (well, the same *type* of food, I haven't quite got to that desperate stage of regurgitating meals yet).

Now there is nothing unusual about eating the same meal two days running. It's often the most practical solution when you're travelling alone and when certain items are on special offer, or too big for one meal, but this was the first time I had been called up on it.

"You had that meal last night, didn't you?" Said a youngish lady, in a very smug, matter-of-fact way. She was clearly very proud of her high-grade detective work.

"Erm, yes..." I tentatively replied. A little taken aback by her sharpness.

"Thought so."

She walked away, evidently satisfied by the outcome of the exchange. I in turn gingerly returned to the important task of jabbing my broccoli in the saucepan, having made a mental note to be more cautious about who may be tracking my eating habits.

What did amuse me though, was that when I arrived in the kitchen at the *same* time, and with the *same* food as yesterday evening, was the sight of the woman next to me. She had also been there the previous evening, at the *same* time, using the *same* ingredients. She was even using the *same* hobs! (Which she had left turned on *again* after she was finished I might add. Tsk tsk.) At least I had the decency to wear a different t-shirt!

She was unbelievably French looking too. She was very slight, she probably had a stripey top on, she was *definitely* wearing a beret (possibly the only real French feature about her in reflection, but I'm still going to have my moment so I don't care what you say) and I'm pretty sure she was cooking garlic. She *certainly* had onions growing off her armpits.

I would have said some 'witty' comment to her, but my French is limited in terms of cooking talk or coincidences, so instead I just smiled stupidly (not for the first time this trip) and began chopping my broccoli.

Anyway, you can imagine my disappointment when I overheard her twenty minutes later being English – ruining the stereotype for everyone. I suppose that just proves that you can never judge a person by their (ridiculous) bumbag.

An hour later I was interrupted whilst writing - well, this journal thing - when a Dutch girl nearly attacked me after I admitted that I hadn't tried 'L&P'. I didn't even know what it was! I assumed it meant 'Lipstick & (fake)Pearls' judging by the way she was turned out, but after running off upstairs, she soon returned with what turned out to be some reasonably dull tasting lemonade. Thank god I met her.

Time to move on I think…

Chapter 12

Volcano Climbs and Cocktail Limes
Thoughts of a Card Playing Protest Leader

Day 97

South America

The longest day.

Many people drag themselves into work on a Monday morning and moan about how quickly the weekend went, wishing that Saturday had lasted a little longer. Well, today I experienced what that would be like, and to be honest I'm quite looking forward to a change. So far Saturday has been going on for over thirty hours, and it's not done yet.

I thought that there might be some kind of sonic boom, or exciting in-cabin lighting display to mark the crossing of the International Date Line, but in actual fact there was nothing. It was a little disappointing. They didn't even bring round any celebratory peanuts. This may be because the date line has been skewed to avoid travel confusion and to accommodate things like Hawaii, or it could be because it's not the big deal I'd like to try and claim it is. I'm not even sure when we crossed it, except that it was probably sometime during 'She's Just Not That Into You', which I can now confirm is a chick flick, and not a very good one.

As a result the ten and a half hour flight from Auckland to Santiago was pretty uneventful, although that's probably a good thing as there are limited eventful incidences involving flying that can be anything other than negative.

One issue that *did* slightly limit my enjoyment of the flight however, was the message delivered to us at the safety briefing stage of the flight that asked us to switch off any remote control toys that we may have. This was terrible luck, as I often use the uncluttered centre aisles of long-haul flights as my chosen test track for radio-controlled cars. Air travel is all restrictions these days.

I had a nice ending to my time in New Zealand, with a fun exchange with an airport customs employee as I made my way into the departure lounge.

"Sorry, can I just ask what you've been keeping in that water bottle?" The softly spoken man politely asked after scanning my carry-on bag.

"Water." I replied. Hoping he didn't think that I was simple, or that I was just relaying half of the question in a poor attempt to hide the fact that I was actually harvesting a small army of highly trained worker-bees to assist me in my takeover of New Zealand.

"Ah, okay. It's just that some people have been filling them with fuel."

"Oh. No I'm not so keen on the taste." I flatly responded.

He laughed. This was the first customs officer I had been able to have a joke with, and it was a nice end to a country whose people I had found to be very astute and engaging. It was also encouraging to know that there are some conscientious air passengers that have the foresight to bring fuel reserves in case the plane has difficulties with its own.

The following day (which was actually the same day) we landed in Chile's capital, with spectacular views across the city and with the backdrop of the Andes mountain range beyond. Actually it was a lot like New Zealand.

After a relatively smooth glide through customs and baggage reclaim I managed to fight my way through the usual rabble of unlicensed taxi operators, withdraw some legal currency, and find my way to the bus stop to catch the bus to the city.

I was buzzing as the bus bumped along the dusty roads. It had been five years since my last visit to South America, and I was very excited to be back in a bustling Latin American culture. The prospect of travelling in a group again was also something I was very much looking forward to.

The twenty minutes of research that I had done at the branch of Borders in Auckland two days ago had proven useful too, as not only had I got the right bus without problems, but I soon even knew which road we were on, and found the right place to get off. Minutes later I was at my hostel, and soon chatting to a flock of Canadians and Americans who were about to start teaching placements in various towns and cities across Chile.

After arranging a dinner date, I ditched my bag in the room and went out in search of some basic provisions, quickly finding a suitable outlet in a side street around the corner from my hostel.

"Una agua grande, sin gas, por favor." It was like I'd lived there all my life!

And before I knew it, in front of me was a large bottle of still mineral water. Native. I mean that *must* have been what the shop assistant was thinking.

That night I went out for dinner with the teachers club, to a nice little restaurant in one of the nearby streets. This was a luxury that I did not have available to me up until now, as eating out was far too expensive for my backpacker budget, but here the food was as cheap as chips. And *especially* chips. They were even cheaper! So we feasted like kings whilst watching Chile beat Paraguay 2-0 in a World Cup qualifier, before we returned to the hostel where I suspected I would sleep well, having finally completed my thirty-nine hour Saturday.

Day 98

I did not sleep well. Tyler, my six foot six vegetarian dorm buddy does not snore. He does however, emit a terrifying nasal outburst with every exhalation whilst sleeping, and this was what kept me awake between four and eight this morning. It also went some way to explaining the dreams I had about hillside sheep massacres.

Day 99

I'm in a hotel! I have a bathroom and a bedside table. I *even* have a lamp! *And* a lampshade! In just over an hour I will be meeting up with the rest of the group that I will be going on this South American journey with. A journey that will see us travel down through Chile, across into Argentina and onto Uruguay, before heading into Brazil and going up the coast to our finishing point - Rio de Janeiro.

I spent yesterday exploring the vast, sprawling urban mass that is Santiago. Tyler and one of the American's, Aaron, had asked if they could tag along with me in my day of exploration. Presumably because they thought I was cool and they liked my shoes and haircut. Aaron is one of the group about to start a teaching placement, and I think he will make a good teacher, as he knocked on my door on the dot of 9.30am as he had told me he would the night before.

Now I know I moan about people who laze about in bed all day, wasting the opportunity to see these fantastic places you visit when travelling - but c'mon! I hadn't slept in two days and Tyler's respiratory eruptions had left me a little shaken from the night, so an extra hour in bed would have been nice.

But in true British fashion, I denied that I had been asleep, and we set off. Well I showered, put on a t-shirt back to front, picked up my map, cursed, put my t-shirt on the right way round, and *then* we set off. I had other clothes on as well of course. And Aaron wasn't standing at the door while all this was happening either. That would have been inappropriate.

The three of us headed east towards the more central areas of the city, passing through the 'Plaza de Armas' square, before we climbed a big hill in the Santa Lucia district. This is a significant landmark as it stands out as one of two natural high points in an otherwise flat cityscape. It was also an important scribble on my hand-drawn map that signified the rough location of the hotel where my trip would start the following day.

We then made the forty-minute ascent by foot to the top of the second high point, San Cristobal, accompanied by a stray dog that followed us the whole way up. At the top was a large statue of the Virgin Mary, and what would have been impressive views across the city had it not been for the thick smog.

We then made our descent down the mountain on the funicular railway, which jolted us uneasily back to the bottom, before we split up, and I went off to explore some markets.

As I made my way back across the city towards the hostel I came across a much needed cash machine, but when I emerged from the building having withdrawn some Chilean Pesos, I was confronted by a wall of protesters fronted by a large banner blocking the road. This inadvertently forced me in the wrong direction, causing me to have to follow the route of the march *ahead* of the protesters. This was the *opposite* direction to where I wanted to go, but I was left with little choice. It was go their way, or get trampled.

The protesters eventually came to a stop when confronted by a security barrier and military police. I was caught in the middle. The crowds didn't look very happy, and the shouting was getting louder. I didn't really know what to do, so I decided the best course of action was to take some pictures, and then get the hell out of the way by diving down a side street that had thankfully come to my rescue. I'm still not exactly sure what they were protesting about, but I have my suspicions after earlier noticing some posters promoting a McFly concert that was happening in the city that night.

That evening a few of us went out for a meal, and then sat around in the hostel drinking beer and playing cards. This would soon become the staple ingredients of a South American evening.

Something that has always entertained me when travelling in non-English speaking countries is the translation of instructions. There was one such set of instructions in the hostel toilets (a place that isn't always synonymous with entertainment) that requested that you 'do not throw papers down the toilet'. Well I had heard rumours that Chile had serious issues regarding people disposing of bank-robbery blueprints and academic research down the toilet.

Better still though; it referred to users as 'passengers'. I've never thought of myself as a passenger when using the toilet before, but I liked it. It raises the status of the job in hand (steady) and makes the task seem more skilled and significant than perhaps it really is. Mind you, with the tiny space provided it *was* a bit of a mission, and one that involved a lot of bashed elbows, but this sign definitely made the operation seem like more of an achievement, like I was some kind of cubicle crusader – on a quest to...well, you can see where this is heading.

Today's important task was to obtain the 'local payment' for the impending tour. This wouldn't have been such an issue had the payment been required in a reasonable currency, but no, they wanted it in US Dollars. I had English Pounds, Euros, Australian Dollars, New Zealand Dollars, Chilean Pesos...I even had some United Arab Emirates currency for some unexplained reason, but no sodding US Dollars.

I eventually managed to track down a cash machine where I then had to transvert (yes, I think you'll find that's the correct term for what I did) Chilean Pesos into English

Pounds in my head, and *then* into US Dollars. I then withdrew what I thought was enough Chilean Pesos, and tracked down the currency exchange office I had spied earlier in the day, and approached the counter to make the switch.

Part of the fun of travelling is getting by in countries where you don't really speak the language. Sadly I think the cashier I dealt with did not see it in the same way that I did, and was showing signs of exasperation at my continued presence while we interacted through post-it notes and the lost art of hand-signals. I eventually managed to establish with him what it was I wanted, and in turn how much Chilean currency I needed to achieve this. He looked visibly relieved when I finally left ten minutes later, dollars in hand.

Unfortunately I later discovered that I *hadn't* got enough dollars, but not wanting to inflict any more pain on that particular employee (and I was now based on the other side of the city and couldn't be bothered to trek back over there) I set off to find another place that offered the service. It was then that I discovered the 'Two Streets' rule*.

I walked into a bank and enquired in my fantastic pigeon-Spanish about the whereabouts of a money exchange facility, and was told (confidently I might add) that there was such a place two streets down on the right hand side. I thanked the lady, and followed her directions. It wasn't there. I then went into a small supermarket and asked the gentleman behind the counter the same thing, and once again I was told there was a relevant outlet two streets down on the right hand side. Right. So I set off further down the road, and still there was no sign of it. *Eventually* I found the place. It was a further *five* streets down and on the *left* hand side.

The 'Two Streets' Rule: If you ask someone in a shop (or similar) where another building or place is, that person (if they actually don't know where it is) will tell you that it is two streets away. This sounds like it is near enough so that you are grateful for being told that you are close, and therefore show them a large amount of gratitude accordingly. Then, when you discover that they were in fact lying, you are far enough away from them that you don't bother to go back and tell them how wrong they were, and that in retaliation you are going to stand outside their shop and Morris dance in your underwear in order to scare off all of their potential customers.

Day 101

So the night before last we finally all met up as a tour group. We gathered in the reception at Hotel Riviera, where having introduced ourselves, we immediately forgot everyone's names, and then completed the necessary administration before we went out for a drink. At an Irish bar. Logically.

After a few drinks mixed in with some classic travelling; "Where are you from? Where have you been travelling so far? What's your shoe size?" line of questioning, we boarded the city's subway system and rode across the city to our tour guide Christian's brother's flat. As you do.

We then spent the rest of the evening drinking and getting to know one another, before heading off into the night to make our way back across the city to our hotel, accompanied by an ever-increasing entourage of stray dogs. It's a good indication of how far you've walked by the number of dogs you gain on the journey. That night we started with zero, and arrived with six. We picked up a new dog roughly every five minutes. You can do the maths.

Yesterday a group of us went for a wander around the city, before we all met up again in the evening to go back to Christian's brother's flat (quickly establishing itself as the unofficial Chilean tour HQ) where we watched films, ate, and drank some more. We then got a mini-bus to the main bus terminal, and boarded our first night bus (complete with reclining seats!) to the town of Pucon, eleven hours south of Santiago.

Now I've never been very good at sleeping on buses, and god knows I've had time to practice. I must have racked up well over a hundred hours of bus-time on this trip so far, yet I have still to master the art of losing consciousness in my seat. Often the spectacular landscape is a welcome distraction, but on these night buses they close the curtains and turn off the lights so you have little alternative than to close your eyes and hope for the best.

Sadly this didn't work, and the wonderful snoring from the lady in the opposite seat did little to assist, but I did eventually drift off nine hours into the journey, just as my 'breakfast' was dumped on my lap, firmly waking me up again.

Day 102

We're now in Pucon, a quaint little lakeside town in the Andes.

After arriving yesterday morning we took a walk around the town, getting something to eat in a small restaurant in the town and messing about by the lake.

We returned to the wooden house where we were staying later that evening, where we cooked dinner and then played cards and drank. This was by now the default set-up for a GAP Tour evening. I got to bed around half past one, but only got five hours sleep as my bed was in the *freezing* outhouse, and the early morning shower did little to improve things as it flicked irrationally between scorching hot and ice cold.

There wasn't much time to worry about this though, as today we had an activity planned. Yesterday we had been shown a highly professional laptop presentation of the different activities on offer in Pucon, and everyone had agreed we should climb the local volcano. But then these things *always* seem like a good idea when you're sitting in a wooden cabin by an open log fire.

So here we were at six in the morning, loading up on cereal bars and crudely slapped together sandwiches and about to embark on what we were told was a casual stroll up a hill. Maybe we should have sussed something when we were handed cramp-ons and ice picks, but it's just not the backpacker way to over think things, and so we collected up our gear, and got in the minibuses that would drive us to the starting point.

Twenty minutes later we arrived during a spectacular sunrise at the foot of Volcano Villarrica. The stunning views of this perfectly conical shaped, active, smoking volcano left us looking up at it in awe. Well, those of us that weren't too hung over anyway. We didn't have long to take in the magnificence of this geological masterpiece though, as we were soon stuffing various layers into our rucksacks and sliding on our sunglasses as we began our assent.

We scrambled over rocks and up scree slopes as we followed the ski lifts up the mountainside. As the sun rose and the climbing got steeper we had to shed layers, and slowly the true size of the task started to dawn on us. The guides had led us to believe that this climb was not a big deal, showing us a selection of photos depicting happy trekkers as they bounced along the gravel tracks. It was becoming clear that this was a little misleading, and soon our group began to divide into different groups based on speed, and gradually different members started to turn back. Suddenly the previous night's heavy drinking and minimal sleep didn't seem like the best preparation for such a task.

After three hours of hard trekking, our group arrived first at the snow line. Here we paused to attach cramp-ons, gaitors, helmets and to detach our ice picks and shove a sandwich down our necks. I also took the opportunity to take a sneaky whiz behind a rock. This was easier said than done, and having strategically positioned myself behind a rock, I then began sliding gracefully down the slope mid-stream, just finishing up as another climbing team appeared from round a lower rock formation. This was probably a less than motivational sight for them.

We learned that we only had until 2pm before we would have to turn back to ensure we were off the volcano by nightfall, so our group of four – 'Team Summit' (Gavin, Alex, Charlie and myself) left for our bid to make it to the top.

After a twelve second briefing from the guide we ploughed up onto the ice, having to adjust to using the cramp-ons and ice axes for stability as it got much, much steeper. The glare off the surface was blinding, and the crisp ice put a lot of strain on our ankles.

As we zig-zagged up the forty degree slopes we had mixed feelings; On one hand we had the summit towering above us, never seemingly getting any closer, whilst on the other side we had the stunning views out across the mountains, with Pucon and its neighbouring lake far below.

Time was getting tight, and we were struggling with muscular injuries and motivation. Gavin had developed cramp in his legs, but his imaginative and diverse array of profanities in response to this was conversely energising, which was much needed as the surging boost of the tic-tac I had indulged in two hours ago was beginning to wear off, and my underwear was visiting regions that would void any returns policy. On we trudged.

Then suddenly, at 1.30pm we dragged our weary legs over an icy ridge...and there it was! The huge, gaping crater of the volcano lay right there before us. We had done it! It was a fantastic feeling. Here we were standing on the edge of an active volcano – the most volcano shaped volcano you could ever have drawn as a six year old in a geography lesson. It was even smoking.

We had just enough time to take in the breathtaking views out across the Andes and to take a few photos of 'Team Summit' in some pop band poses before we had to begin our descent back down the volcano.

With the satisfaction of having made it, the journey down was far more relaxed. This was helped by the fact that it was possible to slide down the ice, although it was slightly dangerous as it risked falling off the mountain in numerous places, and once you started sliding, it was hard to stop. I think we probably all felt pretty invincible by then though, so we did it anyway.

Once down onto the lower rock slopes we were able to scree-run down the slopes, but this proved tricky too, and we collectively tumbled over several times. As a result we were all left with a stylish dust-tan on our return to the mini-bus, having made it down from the summit in just under two hours.

Another evening of drinking followed our successful ascent of Volcano Villarrica, accompanied by a barbeque back at the house-hostel. Large slabs of steak were mercilessly prodded and poked in-between swigs of beer as we discussed the day's adventures, before everyone gradually slipped off to bed to get a few hours of recovery before the next day's activities.

The following morning we were up at a more reasonable hour, and we were soon happily swanning around in our speedos, because today we were going white water rafting!

This had seemed like a good idea when we were choosing activities to do the other day, but having climbed a volcano yesterday it didn't quite feel like such a smart move. But as we've established, travelling isn't about thinking *or* being sensible, so we grabbed our towels and boarded the minibus once again.

After half an hour of bouncing along dusty roads we arrived at the starting point. Here we were kitted out with wetsuits, wetshoes, wetgloves, helmets and lifejackets. Oh, and an oar. Although I suspect the oars were more for show, as they seemed to have little impact against the grade 5 rapids that ensued.

A short briefing followed, where we were given instructions on how to sit in the rafts and how to dive across the rafts if the situation warranted it. We then confidently strode off into the river. With the raft, obviously. Soon we were gently bobbing over mini-rapids, finding time between oar-strokes to decide on a suitable celebration in the event of successfully navigated rapids (banging our oar-heads together in a tee-pee formation and shouting was the carefully and democratically selected choice) and then it was time to hit the big boys.

When you're precariously perched on the edge of an inflatable, you can't help but feel exposed as you plummet down waterfalls and into rocks, but after an exhilarating few seconds (where we successfully forgot all the instructions we had been taught in the briefing) we emerged from the rapid triumphant, thoroughly wet, but all intact.

Then we realised that Paula was missing. She had dived heroically across the raft when the appropriate call was given – possibly a little too enthusiastically though, as after a lot of confusion and searching she was found wedged between two rocks at the bottom of the rapids. Well, it was *nearly* a success, and certainly warranted a celebratory oar bashing.

The next set of rapids were more of a concern though, as our raft guide told us to "forget everything we had just been taught", and if we fell out, "swim like crazy" to the riverbank.

Apparently we had fifty metres after these rapids before we went over a waterfall and, well…left an empty seat on the minibus home.

Luckily we survived this test without exploring these consequences, and so we careered on down the river, careering through more grade 5 rapids and with no further casualties. This was more than could be said for the other raft, where everyone blindly followed their guide's instructions to "stand up" as they went over the rapids. Needless to say they all fell out, and probably felt quite stupid afterwards, if not a little damp.

Soon it was all over, and we were safely back on dry land and eating nibbles.

That night we made caipirinhas, the hugely popular South American cocktail, and we started playing drinking games.

Suddenly, 'Team Canada' (aka Alex and Paula) sparked up. And by that I don't mean they started smoking. That would be reckless in a wooden house. No, instead they brought a set of plastic cups to the table, and soon we were taking part in our first game of 'flip-cup'.

The idea of the game is to line up in two teams either side of the table. You each have a cup and fill it with as much drink as the person opposite you. Then, starting at one end, you down your drink and have to flip the cup upside down from the side of the table. Once you've done it, the next person goes, and the first team to finish – wins! It was a massive hit.

A few hours later, and after a lot of shouting, cheering…and of course drinking, we headed out to a salsa bar. We then found ourselves salsa dancing into the early hours…or at least attempting to, and also doing tequila shots as it later emerged. I blame these for my sudden fascination with the swivel door that led off to the toilets, which I'm pretty sure I spent a good half hour demonstrating to people how to walk through with dignity. The irony was not lost on me the following day. The problem was that I kept then appearing in the toilets and then walking out again, much to the bemusement of those using the facilities. At least this confirmed that I was going into the *male* toilets, and I still maintain it was a novel and exciting toilet entry system.

After a couple of hours sleep we were up early (*again*) for an eight-hour bus ride to Puerto Varas. An eight-hour bus ride that was less than pleasant given the previous night's antics, but thankfully we all made it, in…*reasonable* health.

* * *

I'm now in a room with a view! I can see out across a lake to a snow-covered volcano (in case there hadn't been enough of these in recent days) from my third floor residence. Sadly this means that there are three flights of stairs to climb, which after two days of strenuous activities, my legs are less than impressed with.

Yesterday evening we went out for a meal at a seafood restaurant, where we ate…seafood, surprisingly. We also had some nice hollow pastry things that we filled with a salsa dip.

Afterwards a few of us went on to a bar to play some pool. Here we met another tour group that was doing the same trip as us but in reverse. They quickly managed to establish themselves as a disturbing group of individuals, an after beating them at pool we headed back to the hotel, very happy to have the fun and friendly group that we did.

This evening we plan on – you guessed it – drinking at the hotel, before the next day's lengthy bus journey across the border...

Chapter 13

Steak Knives and Bus Rides
Thoughts of an Argentinean Golf Professional

Day 107

The night of a thousand steaks.

It's a cold, dark, rainy June evening, and it's raining. It's also dark, and pretty cold. And it's June, so that's probably clarified all of that. More significantly though, we're now in Argentina!

Having had a much-needed strum on the resident guitar, and having completed the important task of trying (and succeeding!) to fit four people into the bag lockers in our room, everyone seems to be writing in their journals and so I think I'll join them. Not writing in *their* journals obviously, but in mine.

We were back at the bus station in Puerto Varas yesterday morning, and a few of us were kicking a football about as we waited for the bus that was late. When it did finally arrive, a reasonably uneventful seven-hour journey ensued. The only moments of any significance being the border crossing, or cross*ings*.

It was dark, and I had been telling one of my fellow travellers, Mark, a joke when we pulled up at the Chilean border. Here a border control officer got on the bus and asked us if we were feeling okay. It was nice of him to care, but I think he was probably checking (albeit not that thoroughly) if we were stealing illnesses from Chile.

Once satisfied with our collective 'yes' and after a quick stamp of our passports we were back on our way. What was strange was that it was a further forty minutes of driving before we arrived at the Argentinean border, where we were submitted to bag checks and another round of passport stamps. I have no idea of our official location between these two points, as technically we were not stamped into any country. I like to think that we were lawless! As a result I feel a little disappointed that we didn't make better use of this period.

Anyway, once we were officially back in a country, I continued with my joke. It may have been a long joke, but dragging it out over an hour and a half so that I could claim it was an 'international joke' – thus making it seem far more superior to your usual 'domestic comedy' – seemed to have little effect on Mark, and to be honest he looked like he wanted to hit me by the time I had finished. He soon calmed down though, and then I was able to kick back with a tic-tac until our arrival in Patagonia.

It was late evening when we arrived in Bariloche. We had seen snow on our journey in, but now we were faced with pounding rain, and pounding cold, and we were all very much looking forward to giving our stomachs a pounding with some of Argentina's national delicacy – steak!

After ditching our bags at the hostel, we set off into town to track down a suitable meatery, and it wasn't long before we were seated and tucking into some excellent cow. That morning I had decided that we had been together as a group long enough for me to reveal that I could have quite a significant appetite, and had demolished five pieces of breakfast cake. In my defence they kept putting their slices on my plate (as they chose the slightly more unfamiliar vodka-breakfast combination) and I hate to see waste, *especially* when travelling and on a budget – you have to take anything you're offered!

That evening proved another opportunity to demonstrate my deceptive stomach capacity, and after finishing my half-kilo of steak, I was offered a selection of other people's cast-offs. Being hungry, I ate it up willingly. It was estimated that I ate around 1.3kg of steak that night. Suddenly I had a reputation.

Bariloche is famous for having South America's finest chocolate, so we spent today out and about visiting some of the town's many chocolatoriums. Each outlet had rows of glass display units filled with a huge selection of chocolates. The nicer establishments even gave us free samples! These shops had a very Christmassy feel to them. In fact the whole town did, probably helped by the fact that it was the beginning of the snow season, and the mountains were stocking up accordingly. I'm not sure why this makes it Christmassy though, I mean I couldn't tell you the last time *I* experienced a white Christmas. I think I've just fallen victim to the children's film ideal. I never did get a Turbo Man, even though Arnie managed to convince me every year without fail that it was all I wanted. Growing up was tough.

Day 109

Our second day in Bariloche involved another climb. We had been told that there was a mountain with nice views out across the lakes that was a short bus ride away, so a slightly altered 'Team Summit' was up at the break of dawn - well, around nine thirty - to take on the challenge.

We found the bus stop with minimal hassle, and we were soon rumbling along the lakeside road. After a brief chat with a Jehovah's Witness we found directions to god... I mean the base of the mountain, and we were soon scrambling up the maze of upward paths, casually tripping over fallen branches and rocks.

After a not too demanding half an hour, we arrived at the top. It was more of a large hill really, but there were still nice views across the snow-capped mountains and lakes below.

A few photographs later and we were sliding back down the hill, and once at the bottom we got on another bus that would take us further along to the lakes where we had been recommended a walk.

We got off the bus at a very posh looking hotel resort, and adjoining it was a very smart golf course. We had a look in the clubhouse, and then (although we were all quite curious and keen) decided that it would be silly to play, so we started on the walk.

Then we realised that we all wanted to play quite a lot, and that in fact we *were* all quite silly, and that it would therefore be very appropriate for us to have a go. So in our scruffy hiking gear, we marched confidently passed the entrance security guard and into the clubhouse.

After stamping mud into the plush carpeting, we stood at the reception desk and negotiated some golf sticks (we shared to save costs) and six balls, and then we set off onto the first tee.

Now this first tee happened to be in full view of the clubhouse, and although the rest of the course was deserted, we felt we should give the impression that we had a dignified and professional approach to golfing – just in case anyone *was* watching.

Luckily we all rose to the occasion, and if anyone *had* been watching those first four shots, they wouldn't have had any idea of the club-swinging chaos that would ensue.

Balls flew all over the place - into trees, lakes, and occasionally onto the fairway. It was hugely fun though, and we spent a good three hours bashing divots into this professional golfing venue, as the clouds above switched between spitting out rain and sunshine.

By around half past five we decided that we were all probably professional golfers, and that it was getting dark and cold, and that the rest of the group would probably be wondering where we had got to. So we deposited our golfing gear, and made our way back to the town on the bus, where we group-cooked again (cooking those members of the group that were laziest) before going to bed as we had a long bus journey the next day. Well *obviously* we drank and played cards first.

Today's bus journey was one that would see us travel right across the width of Argentina to the nation's capital – Buenos Aires. The bus was the nicest we had been on, and this was handy as it was also the longest at twenty-one hours. It only had three seats in a row, and they reclined to an almost horizontal position. We were even treated to a three-course dinner (albeit at two in the morning) that was served with champagne and on a lap tray. That's right – a *lap tray*! Luxury indeed.

I was lucky enough to have the added bonus of an upstairs front row seat, giving me uninterrupted views of the impressive Patagonian landscape, and of the irregular road markings that made weaving around the tight mountain roads a little disconcerting. However, this was nothing compared to the alarming sight of seeing a large pipe coil fall off the back of a truck as we travelled behind it at over eighty kilometres an hour, and then the even *more* ludicrous sight of the truck reversing down the highway to retrieve it. After this I decided to close the curtains and listen to the insightful observations of fellow travellers, Noleen and Jess.

Day 111

Splendid! ...is the name of the hotel that we now find ourselves in. Sadly it doesn't quite live up to its name. Hotel Shoddyandfallingapart would be a little more appropriate. Its predominant negative features include the collection of door handles that fall off when touched (they would be fine if they were decorative, but the very nature and necessity of door handles is based upon them *being* handled) and so we often find ourselves prying at the lock to get into our rooms.

Another issue is the floor numbering system. The ground floor is labelled accordingly, but they have numbered the second floor — floor 1. I have no idea what the floor in between is called.

My main annoyance and reasoning for highlighting this discrepancy is that while I raced up the stairs to beat my roommates; Emma, Susie, Mark and Charlie, up to our room on the fifth floor (while the four of them rode in the dodgy three-capacity lift) I found myself having to run up an *extra* flight of stairs as there was an *extra* (unexpected) floor, which meant it was a an *extra* close race, and so I had to make an *extra* effort and commit to a diving finish that left me with an *extra* (and would-be unnecessary) carpet burn. I mean really. It's just irresponsible of the hotel to allow this to happen. They should re-number their hotel floors as a result, to prevent a similar incident from re-occurring. And you just *know* it will.

I'm now not sure if winning was worth the carpet burn in the end, but then travelling is all about sacrifice.

We spent our couple of days in Buenos Aires exploring the city from our central location. Everything was on our doorstep; shops, markets, restaurants, big pink government buildings...you name it! There was even a '25 hour' convenience store in the next block down from our hotel, just in case you were in desperate need of supplies during an extra long day.

Last night we went out for the last group meal of the first leg of our trip, as here we would lose some of the group, and gain some new members. It was an evening of sadness and nostalgia in regards to how far we had all come together (approximately 3000km as you ask) but also celebrating what a great trip it had been, as well as the anticipation as to what the next group would be like, and looking forward to where we would be heading next. I even got a free litre bottle of beer for finishing off other people's meals after some of the group told the waiter to put their leftovers on my plate. I failed to see a downside in that challenge...

However, all these issues risked overshadowing the important and exciting feature of the hotel pillows. They were imaginatively encased in 'pillow-sleeves'. These are crazy times for sure.

Chapter 14

Gaming Halls and Waterfalls
Thoughts of an Off-Road Buggying Rainbow Chaser

Day 115

After a few days in the Argentine capital, the new-look tour group set off in our usual convoy of taxis, but this time it was to the port.

A three-hour ferry trip across the Rio de la Plata to Colonia in Uruguay followed, during which we bonded as a new group through the familiar method of card playing, and more specifically, the number one card game played whilst travelling – 'shit head'. *Everyone* has different rules for this game, and after four months of playing numerous variations of it I now have absolutely *no idea* what any of the cards mean.

It was fun all the same though, and it passed the time, as well as allowing us to get to know each other. Travelling is *all about* learning and forgetting names.

We soon arrived in Colonia, and after a short taxi ride we turned up at a nice little hostel where our rooms were spaced around a pleasant inner courtyard. We then set off for the usual routine of finding a cash machine.

This proved tricky, as this small town only seemed to have two, one of which wasn't working, and the other wasn't anywhere we were looking for it. Luckily we found a local who did know, and after again having to re-calculate what the exchange rate was for Uruguayan Pesos, we were soon monopolising the ATM, systematically withdrawing large bills that would shortly be irritating the local café waitress as we settled up the payment after a quick lunch.

The reason we had a quick lunch was because we had an activity lined up for the afternoon – we were going buggying! None of us were especially sure of what this meant, but it emerged that it wasn't pinching empty buggies from unsuspecting mothers and climbing in them before joyriding down hills, but *actually* we were hiring four-wheeled, off-road motorised cages.

We spent the next few hours tearing around the picturesque cobbled streets of the town in, visiting an old lighthouse, a beach, and anything else that we could find in a place…a country even, where we had only been for a couple of hours.

Some of us inadvertently found an old stone bull fighting stadium that had been fenced off. It was probably the nature of our transport that put us in the rebellious mindset, but before long we had climbed (less than smoothly) through a hole in the wire fence (next to the 'do not enter' sign) to take a look inside.

It was an impressive structure, although it did look like it could fall on us at any moment, and so we were soon scrambling back through the fence, much to the disapproving glare of a local resident, who probably thought we all warranted a Uruguayan ASBO.

We then went off road, just as we had been told not to do, and then got stuck in the sand, *again* just as we had been told not to do, before heading to the petrol station as we *were* supposed to do. Buggying was *great* fun!

That night we went out for dinner, and I had the 'multicoloured chicken' because it sounded exciting. It was indeed colourful, and more importantly tasty, and so all was well with the world.

We followed the meal up with a visit to a casino, where we were all watched like hawks by security, and most of us left without gambling anything. It was then bedtime, and our beds were very alluring as it was very cold outside. Almost as alluring as the air-cushioned toilet seat. Now that's bathroom luxury!

* * *

Yesterday saw us board a bus to the Uruguayan capital – Montevideo. It was only a measly four hours (barely enough time to take my shoes off!) but we arrived in bright sunshine, and after checking in to the hotel (that from the outside looked like a giant ventilation shaft, but was in actual fact quite plush inside) we set off for our usual mix of cash machines and lunch.

After a swift cafe re-fill, a few of us went off to explore the city, and ended up in an underground entertainment centre where we played a few games of pool.

It was such a successful find that after our usual evening meal we went back for a game of bowling, where we split into two teams and have a show down! But sadly not a Hoe Down.

The competition was intense, but after a frenetic game of mindless alcohol-fuelled cheering, our team came through victorious (even with one less player I might add). We were helped a little by the fact that this rather primitive bowling alley had all the pins on strings, and one pin was always replaced after the first shot, allowing you to hit it twice. We called it the 'Uruguayan 11', because you could score 11 points…and we were in Uruguay. Inventive, I know.

After bowling we hit the pool tables again, and I was asked by a local to play with him (at pool I mean). His name was Marcelo, although he actually turned out to be called Juan Carlos. It didn't matter though, I still beat him.

This must have impressed him too, because he bought me a beer, and then invited me to smoke marijuana and to go and see some nice 'dancing girls' with him. I politely declined. I decided that I just couldn't forgive him for giving me a false name, however nice these dancing girls were. He then asked me if I spoke any Spanish, to which I replied 'chico', roughly translated as 'small boy'. I think that sorted that out.

I finished off an entertaining evening by accidentally knocking the pipe that was connected to the cistern tank of the toilet in the hotel bathroom, and it sprayed me in the eye. Travelling is full of special moments.

The following day I went wondering around the city in the clear blue sky and took in the sights. There weren't any sights. Although I *did* see the brownest sea I had ever seen.

That evening we went out to dinner (shock, horror) where I stocked up on complimentary breadsticks for the upcoming bus journey, and then we went on to a bar where salsa dancing was once again on the agenda.

Inside the bar we played some more drinking games, but due to the lack of a flip-cup arena we played the film star game, followed by a new game brought (literally) to the table by Al, called 'spoof'.

This game involved holding out up to three coins in a closed fist, and then taking it in turns to guess how many coins are being held out in total. Whoever was left at the end lost, and as a punishment had to do a shot of something unpleasant. So inevitably there was a reasonable wobble to my walk back to the hotel, and this probably only served to encourage the man I passed in the central square.

"Taxi?" he beckoned enthusiastically. He clearly had no idea of my intolerance towards these. Taxis, not men on streets. Well actually…

"No" I said firmly, shaking my head to make it *infinitely* more convincing.

He paused for a second, and then changed his tact.

"Money?" he asked in a slightly more pleading voice.

I couldn't help but look bemused as this man flicked seamlessly between approaches, combining the two main requests of irritating hustlers. I also had to question (albeit in my slightly blurred state of mind) if he really owned a taxi at all. I may hate taxis, but if I'm offered one that doesn't actually *exist* then that *really* gets on my wick.

I was soon free of him though, and had a pleasant stroll back to have a sleep before – you guessed it – another bus journey!

Day 118

Oi!...which is Portuguese for 'Hi!' That's right, we're in Brasil!...which is Portuguese for 'Brazil!' Okay, that's enough of that.

We left Montevideo after two nights in the Uruguayan capital, and travelled north. Uruguay is very flat. We spent most of the journey playing Monopoly on Jane's ItouchPod.

After eight hours on the bus we arrived in the small border town of Salto. Now there isn't very much you can say about this place, and we only stayed one night. I think this exchange sums up our visit to this Uruguayan border town best;

"Excuse me. Who are you all please?" asked a very concerned looking lady at the bus terminal as we collected our bags from the bus.

"We're on a tour across South America." replied Jane.

The lady looked completely baffled.

"Oh. But…why Salto?!"

After eventually deciding *not* to purchase 'Retard' pills from the local chemist - despite my fascination with them and the effects they might have - we were off again in a taxi convoy over the Argentine border to catch a night bus to Brazil.

This involved a covert operation, as we were told that there were substances you were prohibited from taking over the border. Nervously we stood there as the customs officers spent an age scanning our passports, but eventually we were cleared to drive on. I sighed a big sigh of relief as it became clear that I had successfully smuggled contraband into Argentina.

What was it I had? Drugs? Weapons? Illegal immigrants? No. I had a sandwich. In case I got hungry on the long bus trip. Apparently no fresh meat was allowed over the border, so my ham sandwich was technically illegal. I'm now an international sandwich smuggler – so watch out!

The night bus was not the nicest experience. After the luxury of the Argentine buses, this journey was a rude awakening to how different buses in different countries can be. It quickly became clear that all of our bags were not going to fit into the double-decker coach's luggage compartment, and so after a heated discussion in Spantuguese, it became apparent that we were going to have to bring all of our backpacks onto the bus with us, and cram them into the isles. What made this less appealing was that the bus was full of people who didn't seem to like the look of us, and we were very much the centre of attention.

A tense journey followed as they quickly turned out all of the lights, and our bags were constantly watched and scrutinised by our fellow passengers. A few years ago I had been on buses in Ecuador where people had things taken from their bags whilst they had them on their backs, and so we were aware that this wasn't an ideal scenario. The blocked aisles also meant that getting to the toilet was a little tricky, but at least they didn't have livestock freely wandering through the aisles as has been known to happen on other buses.

We arrived at our stop after a disturbed night of loud South American snoring and constant bag readjustment. We grabbed our bags (that didn't *feel* any lighter that when we had put them on) and then got off.

After a few seconds of confusion, we got back on the bus, as it turned out we *hadn't* yet arrived at the right place. Thankfully they put on a video of the 'biggest hits of the eighties', and so the rest of the journey positively *flew* by.

Eventually we *did* arrive in the right place – we were in Brazil! A quick glide through customs and a short mini-bus ride later and we were at our hotel in the border town of

Foz de Iguaçu. There wasn't a lot of time to get sorted out though, as some of us had chosen to do an excursion for that afternoon.

We were told that South America was home to a renowned black market, at which you can get heavily discounted electrical goods. This very much appealed to some of the group, but what appealed to me was the fact that this 'black market' was in the imaginatively named, Ciudad del Este (East City) in Paraguay (or more specifically Eastern Paraguay, surprisingly!).

That's right, this meant another country! And being the sad border-hopping, rack-up-as-many-countries-as-you-can kind of guy I am, I leapt at the opportunity.

So we were soon back on the mini-bus and heading back to border control. I say border control, but there isn't a lot being controlled here. People piled passed the mini-bus windows holding various crudely constructed knickknacks and refreshments as they tried to secure some income.

We were told that they don't stamp your passports here as that can cause complications when returning to Brazil (for Americans mainly) and they want the financial gain from tourist money. This was a little disappointing, as by now many of our passports were looking quite colourful, but we pressed on regardless, and soon we were in the heart of the bustling border city.

It was a bit of a scramble as we got off the minibus and pushed our way through the bombardment of street sales people. We finally made it across the road to the relative safety of what appeared to be an indoor shopping centre, where once we had past the security guards and got inside, we began trawling through the shops.

To be honest there wasn't a lot to this place, and despite numerous swift calculations we established that it wasn't even particularly cheap. The only really point of interest was when we passed a brightly lit outlet that had ladies perfume next to an assault rifle in one of its glass display cabinets. An interesting juxtaposition I thought.

We decided that we didn't need the hour we had been given to explore this bleak, illegal hot-spot, and so we went outside for some fresh air.

There was no fresh air. It was filthy air, and filled with the shouts of angry sales folk trying to swarm us with what can only be described as irrelevant crap.

I mean, how surprised and disappointed can that man *really* have been when I told him that I wasn't looking to purchase a fishing rod?

We therefore decided that going back inside the shopping centre was the best option, and we quickly found a canteen where we sat down and spent the rest of the time playing Uno.

It was then soon time to get back on the minibus for another short (if congested) trip back to Brazil, having crossed into four different countries in the last twenty-two hours.

There is only one reason, and one reason only why we are in Foz de Iguaçu, and it isn't black markets or fishing. This is the nearest city from which to explore Iguaçu Falls, also known as Iguazu Falls, or even Iguassu Falls (depending on which side of the falls you're on, and therefore which country you're in).

However you spell it, this waterfall *is* apparently a candidate for one of the 'New Seven Wonders of Nature', and is one of South America's most spectacular tourist destinations.

Yesterday we crossed back over the border to see the Argentine side of the falls, and what a sight it was.

Our first view was as we approached from the river, powering up the Rio Igua in a speedboat before being taken underneath some if its two hundred and seventy five drops. It was made more spectacular by the fact that we had just done a nature drive in an off road truck, observing trees in their natural environment. Now I don't mean to sound negative, but being blasted in the face by millions of tons of water was a much more dramatic and effective way to experience the power of nature.

Once we had climbed off the boat and rung out our clothes, we headed out along the walkways to view the waterfalls from the top. It was pretty good from up there too. The walkways cleverly weaved along the top of the rocks, and out across the mass of water waiting to drop over the edge, and right up to the Devil's Throat – the highest and most dramatic segment of the falls. Here the sound of the water was deafening, and enhanced by the horseshoe shape.

The thick mist that masked the vast drop provided the base for numerous clearly defined and expansive rainbows to sprout out of. There was clearly going to be no better location or opportunity to find that illusive pot of gold, and by tracking the spectrums we got *so* close to finding the end and reaping its rewards! I now *almost* believe. The sky then cleared and the sunset gave another late and dramatic twist to this stunning piece of nature.

The following day we went to see the Waterfalls from the Brazilian side, which was equally as impressive. Yes, I think that's a sound and diplomatic conclusion to come to. I also cleverly bypassed the violet throwing up that took place in between these two visits after I experienced twelve hours of food poisoning. That'll teach me to have a different lunch from the rest of the group.
Oh, I hope I haven't tarnished your mental picture of the waterfalls.

Day 123

Once we were satisfied that we had seen Iguassu Falls from every possible angle, and having filled up our camera memory cards with evidence of this, we packed up our gear back at the hotel and set-off for our final night bus.

Twenty four hours of busing followed, which included a fleeting twenty minute visit to Sao Paulo. Well, the bus station at Sao Paulo anyway. It was an uneventful journey, and I even got a reasonable amount of sleep. Sod's Law really – four months of buses and the last major journey is the one where I finally crack bus-sleeping.

From Sao Paulo we boarded a smart private minibus that drove us up the coast and through dramatic forests and winding coastal roads up in the hills.

Four hours and one inaudible film later and we arrived in the coastal town of Paraty, at a fantastic little wooden fort-style hostel on the beachfront. The temperature was finally picking up now we were up in the tropics, and the evening sun meant we could once again go out in shorts and a t-shirt. It even started to feel like we were on holiday, especially as we were nearing the end of the trip.

That evening we went out in search of food, stumbling along the quaint cobbled streets as we re-learnt how to wear thongs. A few stubbed toes later and we found a lively little restaurant in the centre of town where we ate a variety of South East Asian cuisine. Fitting really...in the sense that it wasn't at all...but it *was* much needed and the food tasted good.

We didn't do a lot else that evening as it was quite late by the time we had finished eating, and it had been a long couple of days travelling, and so we headed back to the hostel and played some cards before turning in for the night. Another reason for an early(ish) night was the prospect of a spending time on the beach the next day.

We woke up to clear blue skies and a nice inclusive breakfast. What more could you ask for? A sandy beach. And we had that too! Soon we were all out on the shell covered sands, gazing out across the tree-filled hills and islands around the bay that lay in front of us. It was an impressive sight, but there was something else that got me even *more* excited; there was a volleyball net on the beach!

After some reasonably childlike whining on my part, I eventually managed to get a few semi-enthusiastic people together for a game, and soon we were all chaotically diving about the shell-infested court as we attempted to string a few rallies together. They were normal beach shells by the way, not unexploded bombs, although that would have made the game a little more interesting. Having said that, the shells did cut up our feet, but soon we were so involved in the game that it didn't seem to matter.

We ended up spending most of the day playing volleyball on the beach until our hands and feet were thoroughly bruised and sore. It was brilliant. The sun shone down uninterrupted, giving a less than comfortable pink tinge to some of the group.

Others had opted for a slightly more relaxing beach experience, and chose to spend the day sampling the local cocktails. This may have seemed like the perfect solution to unwind after a busy few days, but then again, starting at ten in the morning may have had its consequences. I still preferred the more active approach to beach life, and somehow got involved in a hole digging competition with a dog. I'm being literal here, although that damn dog could probably talk itself out of a tricky situation far better than me. It dug a bigger hole in the sand too. Stupid smooth-talking, hyper-energetic machine-dog.

It was late afternoon by the time we finally dragged ourselves away from the beach, and after an impressive fish platter lunch...early dinner – or 'dunch' if you will, we headed off into town to have a wander around the shops and markets.

There were a lot of interesting and strange bits and pieces in the shops off the narrow streets, and there was also a lot of touristy crap too, so everyone was catered for.

Someone had recommended a popular ice cream parlour, and so we stopped off to sample its delights. I don't often have ice creams, in fact this was only my second of my travels, and so I think my inexperience at self-service ice cream consumption showed. On the few occasions I have indulged myself I've always liked lemon sorbet...but also mint choc-chip. It was here I discovered that you can't always mix good things and it turn out well.

Now I was hoping that would come out more along the lines of 'you *can* have too much of a good thing', but in actual fact I'm just suggesting that you just take turns in having the good things separately. But that's not such a catchy or succinct moral phrase. Still, the ice cream incident demonstrated that you just can't compete with the education you gain whilst travelling.

We got back to the hostel (now sporting some fashionable travel-bracelets) mid-evening and had dinner. No, I'm *not* skipping time; we just managed to condense lunch, pudding, *and* dinner into a four hour period. Impressive, isn't it?

Despite our streamlined eating schedule, I was still hungry enough (and determined enough) to make the most of the all you can eat pizza they cooked for us at the hostel.

Several beers and belt adjustments later and we were ready to paint the town red. Or blue, green and yellow as is more appropriate for Brazil. There was a festival in town that had seemed like perfect timing as it coincided with our stay, and as a result all the accommodation was booked out and the town was buzzing.

Sadly it was a book festival, and although there was still a lively atmosphere in the streets, we ended up in a disappointing bar full of weirdos. Luckily when you're in a large group you can entertain yourselves, and a few drinking games later and no one seemed to care (or possibly know) where we were.

Day 126

The two nights we spent in Paraty were very enjoyable (despite my self-esteem taking a knock when I fell out of the hammock whilst attempting to pick up my drink from the adjacent table, and then the subsequent ear-bashing from 'Team Southampton' (otherwise known as Lara and Carly) but it was quickly time to move on to our penultimate stop – Ilha Grande!

It was a mere three hour drive further up the coast, and then an hour boat crossing to this stunning tropical island, where we arrived in the cloud and mist to the sight of tropical forests rising steeply up the hills behind a beachside harbour. It reminded me of the opening shots of the Jurassic Park island. Hopefully those annoying children wouldn't be waiting for us at the visitor centre though.

Our bags were taken off the boat and piled onto a cart on the jetty, where they were then pushed the short distance along the paths to our hostel. Why we couldn't just carry them ourselves I don't know, but the local folk seemed happy enough to demonstrate their stacking skills so that was fine.

The hostel was an attractive selection of wooden chalets in a hillside clearing, which even had hammocks outside. (Grrr!)

Once we were settled in we headed out for lunch, even though it was around 5pm, and so once again our meal schedule was in tatters. It was a bizarre little cafe, and the fish that we were served was pretty much just a head and bones, but we ate it anyway, and then spent the rest of the afternoon/evening strolling about the streets that formed the main town and playing pool in a bar.

The following day was cloudy and threatening to rain, so we put on our hiking boots and rain jackets and set off on a hike in the forest in search of the ruins of a prison.

We found it, and yes, there were a lot of jokes about me feeling at home. Inspired.

We also saw lots of trees, a large rock and some water. Classic nature. There was even a small viaduct that I decided to give a short history of in order to liven up the walking experience...although I suspect that they may have sensed that I was making parts of it up. *Especially* when I started to involve the Aztecs.

In the evening we went to the main square by the water front for the fantastic annual event that is Festival Julho! It certainly sounded exciting, but then I thought about it a bit. Festival Julho on Ilha Grande. As tropical and culturally-electrifying as it sounded, I'm pretty sure it translates as 'July Festival on Big Island'. It kind of loses something there I feel.

Despite this (and the fact that according to its name it lasts for a twelfth of the year anyway) it was a fun atmosphere, and Brian certainly showed the islanders how to work a trampoline.

The next day we made a group decision not to pay lots of money for a barbeque on a boat. Instead we had a barbeque at the hostel the night before, and then the next day we went on a cheaper boat that took us to a beach on the other side of the island. They say you get what you pay for, and so I guess it wasn't that surprising that the boat broke down mid-ocean.

But after a short delay while we awaited rescue, we eventually arrived in a small bay, and it was then a ten minute walk through the forest to the stunning Lopez Mendez beach. This was surf territory, and *that's* why we came.

We ran out onto the white squeaky sand, and after somehow acquiring some surfboards and body boards we hit the waves. They were big. We weren't very good at surfing. It was brilliant!

While some of the group lay on the beach in the sun, the rest of us spent the three hours getting thoroughly battered by the strong current and waves, and after a few successful surfs and *far more* unsuccessful attempts, we all gathered up our stuff and made our way back to the boat and returned to base camp, all pretty exhausted.

That evening was another meal out in a smart, leafy outdoor pizza restaurant, followed by a brief return to July-fest and a relatively early night thanks to the day's exertions.

The next day would be the final journey. The final journey to the final destination of our South American adventure. The final journey in *my round the world* adventure.

Hopefully the final bloody bus ride for a while too. That's not really fair actually. I've seen some fantastic sights from the windows of all the various buses I've travelled on, I'm just a little bitter that I never properly mastered the travel-sleep.

Day 132

It was only a couple of hours drive up the coast from where our return boat from Ilha Grande docked, and soon we were entering the hectic sprawl of Rio de Janeiro. I think it was clear that everyone was excited, if a little saddened that for most of us this signified the end of our travels.

After checking into our hotel we went off for one last 'cash machine and lunch' routine. Here we had a warning about the dangers of the city, and were told that you shouldn't go near the beaches before sunrise or after sunset as the favela children come out with guns and rob you.

It is a sad reality for such a fantastic location, and a strange irony appeared when I began to notice the numerous and impressive sand sculptures that stood untarnished on the promenade. These fragile works of art would be preserved, and yet you could be shot for merely walking in the same area at the wrong time. As a result we were advised to get into the routine of always carrying some 'robbery-money' loose in our pocket, just in case we were stopped. This also meant I had to make the tough adjustment to using taxis when we went out at night.

After lunch we walked along the world famous Copacabana and Ipanema beaches to a market. It seemed strangely unreal as we ambled along the promenade with the backdrop of Sugar Loaf Mountain and the hillside favelas.

For our final meal together we went out to a posh 'churrascaria', where you have a selection of vegetables, salad and side dishes to accompany the endless 'meat on a stick' that is brought round by the waiters. This was my kind of eatery, and with this in mind I felt I did it justice. I even had the chicken hearts, although I can't say it's a delicacy I will regularly search the shelves of Sainsbury's for once I'm home.

The following day we all departed the hotel for our own accommodation that we had booked now that the tour had finished. I was in a lovely yellow hostel, where I think they did well to act on the assumption that windows and walking space are overrated.

Some of the group met up again informally (we heard they frown upon wearing ties around here) and went off to the main sights of Rio. We went up the seven hundred metres (alright, we went in a cable car) to the iconic Corcovado (Christ the Redeemer) statue, where we had clear views out across the city, whilst getting in the way of tourists trying to (somewhat sacrilegiously if I'm being honest) re-enact the pose of Christ with his outstretched arms. We also took the cable car trip up the two stages that led to Sugar Loaf Mountain where we watched the sunset. Stunning.

One of the unexpected highlights came when we raced up Rocinha – the largest favela in South America – on the back of motorbikes. We were clinging on for dear life as we charged through the streets, diving in between traffic and people until we reached the top of the hill.

Once we reached the top we visited a local art gallery and a school, from which we could look out over this amazing hillside urban-jungle that is home to over 200,000 people. It was a massive maze of patched together buildings overhanging narrow alleys, and as real insight into the poverty gap that exists in Brazil (one of the most defined in the world) as we could hope to get as Western tourists.

Another few days spent on Copacabana followed, with evenings spent in various bars across the city. I felt strangely relaxed (well, as much as you can when having to carry robber-money around) in these last few days. These last few days that have finally led me here, to the departure lounge in the International Terminal at Rio de Janeiro's airport.

I really wanted to end on as bigger high as possible, and I had a plan! I packed my one and only (Argentinean bought!) shirt in my carry-on luggage, and when the check-in desk *finally* opened, I slipped it on in the toilets and approached the desk.

"Hello, can I have your passport please." Announced the check-in lady, in a chirpy voice.

"Yes!" I replied enthusiastically as I handed it to her. A little *too* enthusiastically perhaps, given her raised-eyebrow-led facial expression. I then smiled excessively as she proceeded to tap some details into the computer.

I then handed over my rucksack accordingly, and once that was all labelled up and on the conveyer belt I made my rather sheepish enquiry. "I was wondering if there was any chance of an upgrade?" I was raising *my* eye-brows this time.

"I'm afraid not." She replied sympathetically, but far too quickly if you ask me.

Dammit! I had gone to the all this effort of checking in *four hours* early and put this bloody shirt on and I got shot down in seconds! I was a little disappointed.

There was to be one last surprise though, and my lack of upgrade made the surprise even more surprising...

As I wrote these final paragraphs of my round the world adventure from my seat at the terminal gate, the muffled conversations of fellow passengers interspersed with the occasional PA announcement was broken by a piercing outcry from across the departure lounge. What drew my attention was that it was someone calling my name! This didn't make sense, everyone else had already left, and I was pretty sure I had no family in this neck of the woods.

I looked up to see my friends from home, Anna and Liz, coming towards me and gesturing wildly. Suddenly I wasn't even sure I was still in Brazil, and my face must have been something worthy of a picture.

After a few frantic exchanges it emerged that Anna and Liz had decided to go on holiday to Rio for a couple of weeks, and they were flying home on the same day *and* on the same flight as me!

Not *only* that, but just to top off this bizarre coincidence (neither party knowing that the other one was in Brazil, *let alone* on the same flight) it turned out that we were all in the *same* row of seats. Sitting *next* to each other. The *three* of us in a row of *three*. What were the chances?! They had even checked in a couple of days before, whereas I had only checked in a couple of hours ago. I mean what were the odds that we would be on the same flight, given all of the thousands of flights to the hundreds of destinations that fly every day, and that we would be in adjacent seats when there were over 350 seats on this plane alone to choose from? If I hadn't been in my end-of-travels semi-comatose state I may have exploded with the craziness of it all. Instead we just chatted about our trips, and then when it was time, we boarded the plane back to England. Back home. On *British* Airways. It seemed fitting.

So after the obligatory record of this massive coincidence was taken (a photo by one of the air stewards, who clearly couldn't quite work out the significance and necessity for three people to want to have their photo taken together on a plane) it was once again time to kick back with some B-list films and cleverly presented food trays. This time however, I was heading for home, and I had the added bonus of having friends from home to talk to as well…

Well, when they weren't asleep anyway.

Epilogue

And so that's it. That's the world done. 133 days, 61 hours on planes, 50 hostels, 47 bus journeys, 19 weeks, 18 passport stamps, 14 days on buses, 12 gondola rides, 10 airports, 9 flights, 8 countries, 7 pairs of socks, 6 holes of golf, 5 onnniooon riiings, 4 tall buildings, 3 parachutes, 2 ferris wheels, and 1 Israeli pop diva concert. And not a French maid in sight.

It's been one hell of an adventure, and one that has changed me greatly as a person...okay, that's not really true. The only really noticeable difference is that I no longer have such a high tolerance of chick-flicks. Now this is a bit of a worry, as the evenings of mindless low-grade Saturday night film scheduling that I occasionally like to indulge in could be ruined, but I suppose at least I now know a few more card games to help pass the time.

Having said that, maybe I *have* learnt a bit about myself, however vomit-inducing and clichéd it may sound.

For example; I've learnt how to deal with tricky situations (polos and post-it notes – never leave home without them), I've tested myself physically (if a freebie is on offer, it's worth jumping off a bridge for), I've tested myself mentally (who expected maths to become a pivotal element in the implementation of a comfortable night's sleep?), I've *even* tested myself socially (a well-bitten lip is sometimes the better outcome), and maybe most importantly of all; never underestimate the enlightening conversational power of a taxi-driver.

So maybe I didn't 'find myself', but luckily I found a lot of other people who were probably *far more* worthy of being found. Not that I'm lost...but I'm guessing you probably are now from reading this.

Basically what I'm trying to say is that travelling is great. You get to see great places, you get to try great activities, you get to meet great people...and well, it's just generally pretty great. So you should do it. Just remember to pack a spare pair of socks and a pack of cards and you're all set.

...Oh, and the airline 'Qantas' is an acronym based on the original area that it served, standing for *'Queensland and Northern Territory Aerial Services'*, and *that's* why there's no 'u' after the 'Q'.

There. I bet that's really been bothering you, so now you can sleep happy, and that makes me glad.

Acknowledgements

Chris would like to thank; the weather (for holding out...*most* of the time), my friends and family (for bothering to read my updates), Alex (for giving me the journal that I used to write all this), Katie (for the emails), Nick (for the comments), the Thai police (for their hospitality), the tour guides (for their guiding and assistance), the bus drivers (for their driving), Danny (for the positive thoughts), the airline pilots (for keeping track of changing time zones), Dianne (for monitoring my word invention), Josh (for the moped trip), Nicky and Liberty (for the not-quite full-moon entertainment), Holly and James (for the card games), Team Sunrise (Jess, Kelly and Jack), David and Tim (for lunch and the harbour tour), Viktor the Postman (for the word-facts), Emma (for the road trip), Alex and Katherina (for the tram trips), Morag (for the insight), Mark (for the table-tennis), Hanna and Lisa (for the...erm, tights), the South-East Asia group (Tom, Ashlee, Nathan, Gemma, Tim, Rachel, Lou, Dave, Hamish, Kylie and Cat), the South America group (Gavin, Fran, Susie, Emma, Mark, Charlie, Lara, Carly, Noleen, Jess, Alex, Paula, Bryan, Annie, Mike, Tricia, Al, Jane and Cynthia), all the other tour and bus groups and everyone else who I met along the way and helped shape my trip. And finally thanks to my Mum and Dad - for staying calm, and for not renting out my room while I was away. You're all great.